KV-370-966

Designing and Implementing Ethernet™ Networks

Second Edition

Books and Training Products From QED

DATABASE

Data Analysis: The Key to Data Base Design
Diagnostic Techniques for IMS Data Bases
The Data Dictionary: Concepts and Uses
DB2: The Complete Guide to
  Implementation and Use
Logical Data Base Design
DB2 Design Review Guidelines
DB2: Maximizing Performance of Online
  Production Systems
Entity-Relationship Approach to Logical Data
  Base Design
ORACLE SQL*PLUS: A User's and
  Programmer's Tutorial
ORACLE: Building High Performance
  Online Systems
SQL/COBOL Application Design and
  Programming
Practical Data Analysis

SYSTEMS DEVELOPMENT

Effective Methods of EDP Quality Assurance
Handbook of Screen Format Design
The Complete Guide to Software Testing
A User's Guide for Defining Software
  Requirements
A Structured Approach to Systems Testing
Practical Applications of Expert Systems
Expert Systems Development: Building
  PC-Based Applications
Storyboard Prototyping: A New Approach to
  User Requirements Analysis
The Software Factory: Managing Software
  Development and Maintenance
Data Architecture: The Information Paradigm
Advanced Topics in Information Engineering

MANAGEMENT

Strategic and Operational Planning for
  Information Services
The State of the Art in Decision Support
  Systems
The Management Handbook for Information
  Center and End-User Computing
Disaster Recovery: Contingency Planning
  and Program Analysis
Techniques of Program and System
  Maintenance

MANAGEMENT (cont'd)

The Data Processing Training Manager's
  Trail Guide
Winning the Change Game
Information Systems Planning for
  Competitive Advantage
Critical Issues in Information Processing
  Management and Technology
Developing the World Class Information
  Systems Organization
Project Management: A Comparative
  Analysis of PC-Based Systems
The Technical Instructor's Handbook: From
  Techie to Teacher
Collision: Theory vs. Reality in Expert
  Systems

TECHNOLOGY

VSAM Techniques: Systems Concepts and
  Programming Procedures
How to Use CICS to Create On-Line
  Applications: Methods and Solutions
CICS/VS Command Level Reference Guide
  for COBOL Programmers
Data Communications: Concepts and
  Systems
Designing and Implementing Ethernet
  Networks
C Language for Programmers
Network Concepts and Architectures
SQL Spoken Here for DB2: A Tutorial
SQL for dBASE IV
Systems Programmer's Problem Solver
CASE: The Potential and the Pitfalls
Open Systems: The Basic Guide to OSI and
  its Implementation
An Introduction to Data and Activity Analysis
DOS/VSE/SP Guide for Systems
  Programming: Concepts, Programs,
  Macros, Subroutines

THE QED INDEPENDENT STUDY SERIES

SQL as a Second Language
DB2: Building Online Production Systems
  for Maximum Performance (Video)

For Additional Information or a Free Catalog contact

QED INFORMATION SCIENCES, INC. • P. O. Box 82-181 • Wellesley, MA 02181
Telephone: 800-343-4848 or 617-237-5656

Designing and Implementing Ethernet™ Networks

Second Edition

Bill Hancock

QED Information Sciences, Inc.
Wellesley, Massachusetts

Ethernet is a trademark of Xerox Corporation

DEC, DECnet, DECServer, DECUS, DELNI, DEUNA, DEQNA, DELQA, DELUA, DEMPR, DEREP,DEBET, PDP, VAX, VAXCluster, VAX/VMS, VT and the Digital Logo are trademarks of Digital Equipment Corporation

3Com, 3Plus, EtherSeries, EtherPlus, 3Server are trademarks of 3Com Corporation

VIM is a trademark of Syntax Corporation

Excelan is a trademark of Excelan Corporation

Macintosh is a trademark licensed for use to Apple Computer

MS-DOS and MS-NET are trademarks of Microsoft Corporation

PC Network, IBM, IBM PC, Personal System/2, and the IBM Logo are trademarks of International Business Machines

PDS is a trademark of American Telephone and Telegraph

TransLAN is a trademark of Vitalink Communications

Softcover ISBN 0-89435-366-7 (acid-free paper)

Printed in the United States of America
        10 9 8

Library of Congress Cataloging-in-Publication Data
Hancock, Bill, 1957–
    Designing and implementing ethernet networks.
    On t.p. the registered trademark symbol "TM" is supoerscript following "Ethernet" in the title.
1. Ethernet (Local area network system) I. Title.
TK5105.8.E83H26   1988   004.6'8   88-18617

Contents

Preface

This book is the culmination of many years of fighting, cajoling, and brutally forcing Ethernets to work. Properly. When they are supposed to.

Actually, the whole idea of a book on Ethernet started because of my heavy involvement in the Digital Equipment Computer Users Society (DECUS). Digital Equipment Corporation (DEC) is a major vendor of Ethernet technology, but there is very little information that is produced by DEC or any other company on the trials, tribulations, and tricks to designing Ethernets. DECUS promotes one-day seminars on various aspects of DEC technologies, one of which being a seminar I teach fairly often called "Designing and Implementing PC and Workstation Networks with VAX Systems." I also teach other seminars, but this particular one had a phenomenal amount of people attend and I started getting a lot of questions on "where do I go to get information on Ethernet?" I found that I didn't really ever analyze where I got my information from. I soon found that there was not any one-stop place that contained a reasonable amount of information that a system manager, programmer, systems programmer, network manager, or department manager could go to find needed information on Ethernet. As time has progressed and Ethernet has become much more popular, I have received more and more queries of this type. So, to solve the problem of where to go, I wrote this book.

This book is not the ultimate tome on Ethernet. I also am well aware that there are plenty of people in the world who most likely know a lot more about Ethernet than I. I also know that I have put in my fair share of Ethernets and have learned much of my skills with Ethernet "the hard way." This book is not an academic dissection of Ethernet, replete with mathematical algorithms on packet collision time or other such topic. It is a book on what it is, how it works, where it fits, how to design an Ethernet, how to install it, and how to fix it when it breaks. In short, a practical guide to Ethernet for those of us who have to live with it each day.

I hope that you find this book useful and my writing style to your liking. I do not write in a manner that may be journalistically appealing to the crowd who are hung up on grammatical syntax or proper tense. I am not writing to just anyone. I am writing to you. I also have found that too many technical books are very impersonal and difficult to understand. The computing and networking industries are complicated enough without my adding to the confusion because of difficult-to-understand language. I suppose that my writing style is my act of defiance.

I am always interested in feedback and information on how to make my books, articles, and products better. Drop me a line at P.O. Box 13557, Arlington, Texas 76094-0557 and let me know what you think and what could be improved.

Bill Hancock
Arlington, Texas, 4/30/88

Dedication

This book is dedicated to my wife Margenia, who doesn't understand a lot about Ethernet, but knows that networks and computers are important to me and, that is enough.

Acknowledgments

It is impossible for any book to get "out the door" without the help of many people and friends.

First I need to thank my wife Margenia for her support. I can be difficult to live with when I am working (I'm not easy to live with at other times as well), but she took it all in stride and was a great help in tracking down documents and helping collate information.

I also need to thank my son, Thomas Nelson, for his help with the graphics. I am a complete klutz when trying to draw anything other than a straight line. Tom was a great help in creating visuals from my scribbles and making the Macintosh Plus do what it does best.

I also wish to thank my ever loyal partner and friend Paul Tuthill who helped review this book for technical accuracy and who understands when I am late with things. Which is often.

Many thanks go to Marty Davis, Bob Russo, Bob Branchek, Fred Sanders, Jill Davis, and Debbie Amiel at ERI Training for all their support, help with printing, marketing, and ongoing friendship. This book would not be here if not for you.

Finally, many thanks to you, dear reader. If not for you, there would be no purpose in writing this book.

Chapter One

The Local Area Network Experience

We should be careful to get out of an experience only the wisdom that is in it - and stop there; lest we be like the cat that sits down on a hot stove-lid. She will never sit down on a hot stove-lid again - and that is well; but also she will never sit down on a cold one anymore.

Mark Twain

Introduction

One of the hottest topics in networking is the Local Area Network (LAN). Every major vendor has their own, and all will tell you that it is the best that can be bought. All will tell you that their network can be used in any environment, provides practically anything you want, and can be upgraded to any network you like. And, if you can believe that, they also have swampland in Florida for sale at bargain prices.

LANs are HOT! A Frost and Sullivan survey shows that LAN connection shipments in 1987 were about 384,000. In 1991 the shipment rate is expected to be 9.8 million connections. Obviously this translates to serious money for the network vendor. In 1986 LANs accounted for about $293.2 million in revenue. In 1991 the LAN market place is expected to generate $5.2 billion.

And which LAN is hottest? In 1987, the most popular LAN was Ethernet. How popular? Forrester Research, Inc., claims that Ethernet (and 802.3) comprises 33% of the LAN market with the IBM token ring lagging behind at 22%. Other surveys are even more optimistic about Ethernet. Dataquest estimated that 52% of installed LANs were Ethernet, while 4% of all LANs shipped in 1986 were token ring. While there is a good deal of disparity between the overall figures, one thing is still obvious: Ethernet is very popular and will continue to be so for some time to come.

To properly consider the figures, let's discuss what a LAN is, what kind of components are necessary for one to work properly, functional concerns, installation concerns, and other such useful information.

What is a LAN?

A LAN, by definition, is a network that is in a small (or local) geographic area. There is a lot of dispute as to what, exactly, defines a small geographic area, but most vendors seem content that the total network length does not exceed five (5) kilometers, end-to-end. This means that the idea of running a LAN architecture from Seattle to New York is not within the definition of a LAN. Not that it can't be done, mind you. At that point, however, is the network still a LAN?

LAN size is measured not only by geographic size, but by population. Most LANs do not support over 1000 systems per LAN and most are much smaller (30-250 range). This is due to the primary customer of LANs offices. Ninety percent of all offices in the U.S. have under 30 users (not total personnel, USERS), 98% have under 300, and 100% of all offices have under 3000 users. The average number of users in an office environment is 115, and each office averages a 10'x10' space. Most offices utilize a wide variety of equipment (terminals, printers, file storage, reproduction services, TWX, facsimile, etc.), and most managers want to get maximum productivity out of workers and office equipment as well.

Another facet of LANs is message size. Most offices use short, bursty traffic that varies in size as tasks are done. Most traffic in a LAN environment is 1-100 byte control messages, some moderate messages of 100-500 bytes, and occasional file transfers of 500-100K bytes. Most users are idle much of the time, but when a user wants to use the network, any response time less than two seconds is usually unacceptable.

80/20 Rule

LANs also are the center of a communications premise called the 80/20 Rule. The 80/20 Rule claims that 80% of all communication happens within a given organization and only 20% ever go outside the organizational walls. In the case of LANs, this can translate, easily, to the fact that of 100% of network resources used by the company, over 80% will be used at the local corporate level and only about 20% of all accountable corporate communications will leave a local level. This is easy to imagine. Take your typical PBX system. In most situations, there may only be 2-5 outside trunk lines but there may be 30-50 extensions internally. Most of the calls that will occur, on a whole, will be internal to other extensions, and very few will be to the outside world. This is how the 80/20 Rule works in networks. Most of the traffic in a network will occur between nodes located in the same local area with only about 20% leaving the local area for other nodes or areas. While it is true that not all LANs will conform, strictly, to the 80/20 Rule, practically all will perform the bulk of networking locally, with much less than half of all traffic leaving the local area.

LANs are also the subject of application vs. type. In all situations, the application that will be serviced should dictate the type of network. This also helps explain why there are various types of LAN architectures. It's quite obvious that an office-oriented LAN may not have all the functionality that is required for an LAN controlling several blast furnaces in a steel mill or the robotics needs of an assembly line. As such, various LAN vendors offer various LAN architectures to provide for the needs of the various LAN environments. Wide Area Networks (WANs) do not have the variety of offerings that LANs have, but they do not usually have to concern themselves with the data rates, access times, and other needs of the LAN environment.

Speed, Speed, Speed

Another attribute of a LAN is speed. Most LANs run at speeds over 2 million bits per second (Mbits or mega-bits). Some can go as high as 100Mbits and there are some experimental types (using fiber optics and femtosecond-speed lasers) that can achieve speeds of 10-20 billion bits per second (Gbits or giga-bits). Speed, however, is an elusive thing. Just because a network is capable of sending up to 2Mbits of data does NOT mean that the receiving (or transmitting) stations are utilizing the 2Mbit rate. Each processor on a LAN has speed restrictions on how fast its internal I/O happens and how fast it can send or receive data to its network interface (controller). Even very high speed mainframes may not be able to handle over 1Mbit of data per second, maximum, due to processor architectural restrictions, I/O peripheral speed, processor overhead, operating system overhead, and communications software overhead. Therefore, just because an LAN architecture makes a claim to a certain speed, it is not valid to associate that speed with the actual throughput that will be achieved on any given node or any group of nodes.

So You Think That a LAN is Cost-Effective, Huh?

LANs are also characterized by a fairly reasonable cost to implement. This means that most LANs are architected with cost savings in mind. Most LAN manufacturers know that they cannot charge as much for LAN interfaces for PCs as they can for LAN interfaces on larger systems. They also are well aware of the market pricing threshholds for any LAN interface and software. Most manufacturers try to relate LAN pricing on a "cost per port" basis, similar to the way that manufacturers try to justify terminal ports. In the networking world, one must be careful with such terminology. A "port" on a network could be a single user PC or it could be a mainframe with 200 users on it. A "port" can also be referenced as an individual program being accessed in a networked manner. If this definition is meant, then does that mean that a system capable of handling 200 simultaneous program-to-program connections will have the same "port" cost of a PC? Some vendors think so. If this were the situation and the cost per port was, say $500.00, then the PC would cost $500.00 to implement and the big system may cost as much as $100,000.00 to implement. If that sounds familiar to you, tem may cost as much as $100,000.00 to implement. If that sounds familiar to you, then you see how many vendors price their "ports" on a network: by how many connections can be handled simultaneously. The port cost can also be used to the vendor's favor in a different way. By the vendor figuring out, statistically, how many "ports" a large system can handle and dividing the total hardware/software cost of the LAN capability by the number of "ports," the vendor can generate a best-case per-port cost. The vendor could just as easily say that the average number of connections will probably be at least 50% of the total number of simultaneous ports, but that can be bad for marketing as it does not allow the product to be viewed as cost-effective as compared to other vendor's products. Let's take the figure we used before of 200 simultaneous connections and see how that can be used to the LAN vendor's advantage. If the total cost for the communications software and network hardware was, say, $15,000.00, then the cost per port would be $75.00. If the PC was able to handle three (3) simultaneous connections and its cost for software and hardware was, say, $750.00, then its cost per port would be $250.00. The vendor could also shift the larger system's per port cost by shifting the number of simultaneous connections from 200 to an average of 60 simultaneous connections and the port cost becomes $250.00 per port on the large system. The vendor then claims that the per-port cost for their LAN technology is $250.00 per port, which is less than their estimated $1,000.00 per port for terminal ports. From the cover of things, that seems like a pretty good deal: about a quarter of the price of a terminal interface, full network capability, and it can solve the file transfer problem that terminals need not worry about. If you can believe that one, they also have an oil well deal in Texas that you won't want to pass up.

In the LAN experience, it is impractical to compare terminal port costs to network port costs. In the terminal situation, it is an all-inclusive cost. In the network situation, it takes two nodes with the appropriate goodies to make the network happen. In our case of the PC to the large system, if our only desire was to connect our PC to the main system, our cost would be $15,750.00 for the network hardware and software. Our per-port charge with three ports on each side connected (six ports or three connections) is $2,625.00. That's an awfully expensive terminal port! Even if we had two large systems talking to each other, we still have the problem of communication: it still takes two to tango, as it is said. That means that if we have two large systems, our total cost to implement the LAN is about $30,000.00. Of that $30,000.00, we will probably average about 20 connections simultaneously (unless we have a very active network) which means that OUR per-connection (a connection requires two ports - one on the sender, and one on the receiver) cost is about $1,500.00 and our per-port cost is about $750.00., which is a far cry from the vendor's per-port cost of $250.00! Remember that our per-port cost figures do not count software and hardware maintenance, operations support, and a myriad of other costs that will surface in time.

LANs become cost effective the more that they are used. The less usage they receive, the more expensive they are. Unfortunately, the more that LANs are used, the more

4

overhead they generate on the system and end they up costing more money in the long run. So, for the flexibility and functionality of LANs, you will pay. A lot.

User Installable?

Many LAN vendors claim that their LAN is user-installable. Some actually are, but most are not. Installing a LAN, under most situations, is not a hard thing to do, but the installation must be very methodical and installation instructions must be followed carefully.

In the case of many types of LAN architectures, vendors include LAN installation instructions for many of the components involved if the vendor deems the LAN to be installable by an average system administrator. Unfortunately, what a vendor thinks is often quite a bit different from the actual issues involved with a LAN architecture. Many vendors promote ease of installation and integration, but frequently neglect proper network design procedures, pre-installation testing, thorough installation procedures, testing procedures, and maintenance/troubleshooting procedures. So what may seem pretty straightforward actually turns out to be more than some companies bargain for.

Types of LANs

Most LAN architectures conform to a variety of voluntary network standards that specify methods and protocols for the different layers of the OSI architecture. As we discuss LAN architecture, it will be very obvious very quickly that while the hardware used in the LAN environment usually conforms to standards established for layers 1 and 2, there are very few standard mechanisms for access above layer 2 that are compatible with other network architectures. Therefore, when looking into LANs, you will find a great deal of compatibilities between the hardware components of many LAN vendors. There is little compatibility, however, in any layer above layer 2 in LAN architectures at this time. OSI networks, however, are on the way and will be increasingly popular as networks become more intwined in business. To properly understand LAN architectures, it is useful to understand the OSI model and its purpose in the network world.

What Started All the Rush...

There was a time when there was no such thing as a network architecture. Companies implemented rather rude, crude, and socially unacceptable software and hardware communications solutions without any thought as to layering or to the implementation of an architecture. The idea of layering really took off with the introduction of an international standard called the Open Systems Interconnect (OSI) model by the International Organization for Standardization (ISO) in 1982 (International Standard 7498).

In 1978, the ISO Technical Committee 97 (they're the folks that handle standardization of information technology) started sub-committee number 16 (TC97/SC16) to develop an architecture and reference model that would serve as the foundation for future standards activities. From 1978 onwards, they have worked very hard at providing a flexible, reasonable communications architecture that could be implemented on a variety of systems and provide inter and intra systems communications capabilities in a variety of environments. Oddly enough, TC97/SC16 has not done most of the work on defining the protocols for each layer of the architecture; other ISO committees have done this, using the model specified by TC97/SC16. Even at this writing, all protocols for all layers have not been totally defined yet, but the model still is highly useful in the definition of how a communications architecture is defined.

What do the Layers do?

Applications
Presentation
Session
Transport
Network
Data link
Physical

To understand the OSI a little better, let's examine what each layer does.

As you can see, a diagram of the OSI model is given. You will notice that the model is basically seven tiers, stacked one upon the other, that reflects a certain function at each layer. User data comes in to the top layer (layer seven) and travels through the various layers of protocols until it finally goes out over the transmission medium (hardware). It then travels to the destination node and begins its travel up the layers of protocols on the remote system until it reaches the destination program on the remote system. This same ordeal happens on all communicating systems for the duration of communications between nodes.

The following few paragraphs define the functionality of each layer of the OSI model:

Layer 1 Physical Layer

This is the touch-and-feel layer. The Physical layer provides for the transparent transmission of bit streams from one physical entity to another (or many as in the case of datagram oriented services such as Ethernet).

Layer 2 Data Link Layer

The Data Link layer handles the transfer of data between the ends of a physical link.

Layer 3 Network Layer

The Network layer handles the routing and switching of information to establish a connection for the transparent delivery of data.

Layer 4 Transport Layer

The Transport layer provides for error-free delivery of data and also acts as the control area for quality of service requirements for the selected data service.

Layer 5 Session Layer

Session layer provides the coordination between communicating processes between nodes ("virtual" connectivity).

Layer 6 Presentation Layer

The Presentation layer provides for any format, translation, or code conversion necessary to put the data into an intelligible format.

Layer 7 Applications Layer

The Applications layer allows the end application to communicate with the communications architecture by providing the appropriate communications service(s) to the application.

At each layer, there may be one or more protocols (in the case of layer 2 and above) or communications media (in the case of layer 1) that communicates with a peer protocol or media on the complementary node(s). What this means is that at any level, there can be more than one way to get data to and from the node and the only requirement is that there be the same peer at the destination node that understands what is sent.

For our purposes, most LANs utilize layers 1 and 2 of the OSI architecture. Layers 3 and above are usually defined by a vendor to provide functionality dictated by the vendor's network architecture. In many cases, OSI upper layer protocols are beginning to emerge in vendor products, such as DECnet, and will continue to influence such products.

In any LAN architecture, it is useful to contact the vendor to find out the intricacies of the LAN itself as well as contacting other customers that are using the LAN and its extensions.

LAN Layouts

LANs come in a variety of "flavors," but most tend to migrate to one of three types: bus, token ring, or token bus.

A Bus-oriented Topology

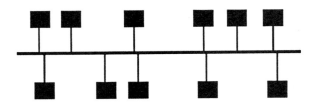

A bus LAN is a network that is configured as a centralized bus with nodes connected off the bus in a "drop" fashion. A prime example of such a network is Ethernet. On an Ethernet, nodes are connected ("tapped") into a centralized backbone cable and communicate to each other using the backbone cable. Through this architecture, systems are easily added without total network disruption. This type of technique is very valuable in areas, such as offices, that need dynamic reconfiguration of network resources in a short amount of time. As a bus topology, Ethernet broadcasts information from each node to the entire network where all nodes listen to transmitted traffic. If a node hears traffic designated for itself, it copies in the packet and sends it up to the host system software. A more thorough discussion of Ethernet follows in later chapters.

A Token-ring Topology

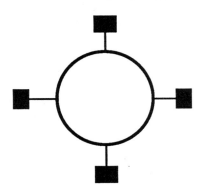

Token ring LANs are nothing more than a ring-topology LAN that allow the various nodes to communicate with each other. The idea is that the source node grabs a free token on the LAN, puts data and a destination address in the token, and sends it on its way. The destination node reads the address, determines if the address is its own, and reads the data if it is. When the token returns to the source, the data is cleared and the token is marked as being free by the source node. There are enhancements to this basic concept, such as the destination node marking a part of the token that the data had been received, multiple tokens on a given LAN, "slots" (groups) of tokens on a LAN, etc., but the basic concept of passing the token node to node is the same. The benefits of the token ring method are an efficient usage of bandwidth, stable behavior during high-load times (this is predictable as the stations are all certain distances away, the queueing delay is constant, and the access times are usually constant), and priority scheduling can be implemented on LANs requiring priority message service, something fairly difficult to implement in the LAN bus architecture scheme. Token rings have problems in that it may take an inordinate amount of time to get a token, they usually require special recovery procedures when a net fails or when the network becomes "confused," it can be difficult to add new stations, and the basic topology of a ring is somewhat unreliable due to a variety of factors. Token ring networks that are popular, however, have managed to overcome many of their drawbacks and allow a great deal of bandwidth over short distances, as well as allowing a variety of nodes and applications to work well in the given environment. Token rings are very popular in the IBM environment, especially in the areas of office automation (IEEE 802.5) and personal computer networking.

A Typical Broadband Token Bus Network

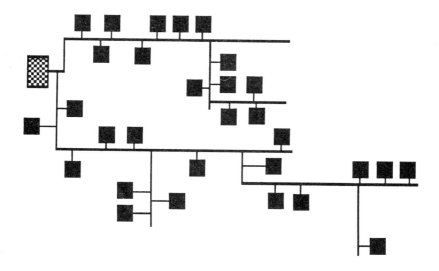

Token bus networks (IEEE 802.4) are, virtually, similar to token ring networks. From a physical point of view, however, they resemble bus topology networks such as Ethernet. In other words, a token bus network looks, physically, like a bus-oriented topology. It functions, however, like a token ring. Token bus networks are useful in that they provide a predictable hardware access time, ease of station addition, priority scheduling of messages, and become more efficient as more stations have traffic to send. They have problems with inefficiency when there is low traffic usage, are complex to initialize, and experience unusually long delays in obtaining token(s) when transferring data to the load of virtual access. If you have been following the industrial automation folks for the last year or two, you are probably already aware that the token bus architecture (IEEE 802.4) is used by the Manufacturing Automation Protocol (MAP) for control of industrial and factory automation processes.

Chapter Summary

In the LAN experience, it is important to not only choose the right LAN architecture for your corporate needs, but also the right upwardly-mobile technology. In the future, LANs will be based on a variety of media, but the most popular will be broadband coax, broadband fiber, and twisted pair copper media. These predictions are not made lightly, but are done based upon known technology vendors, the IEEE, ANSI, ISO, and other organizations are working on. In some situations, a variety of different types of LAN architectures can be run on the same wiring scheme (one architecture type at a time) with a variety of network architectures perched on top of the LAN layer 1 and layer 2 architecture. Therefore, in companies looking into new building cabling, consider the usage of the more popular LAN media, but always consider the up and coming media for future compatibility.

LANs will continue to expand and increase the functionality in the office, manufacturing, industrial, and many other environments, including the home. The International Electrotechnical Commission (IEC) is currently working on a specification (which will most likely be adopted by ISO as an international standard) that will allow a twisted-pair LAN in a home. In the IEC scenario, many appliances and other services (such as voice, medical alert, fire alert, security, Videotex, and others) could be provided on a small, high-speed computer network to control an entire domicile. This can have other implications when considering that the Integrated Services Digital Network (ISDN) can be used to connect the various home LANs into various sites. In the future, it may be very probable that you can send electronic mail to your home from your office LAN or any hotel in the world. You could potentially control appliances remotely (turn on the lights and stereo from Bermuda while on vacation), have a security service monitor your home, have the LAN dial the fire department in case of a fire, and many other services. LANs, while becoming popular, will be the rage in the 80's, 90's and beyond as the price drops and the need for distribution of information becomes more apparent and more necessary.

Chapter Two

Some Insight into Ethernet

Of all of men's miseries the bitterest is this, to know so much and have control over nothing.

Herodotus (484-432 B.C.)

Introduction

If you are reading this book, you have undoubtedly heard something about Ethernet. In this chapter, we shall explore what Ethernet is and some of the basics necessary to understand its place in computing and networking.

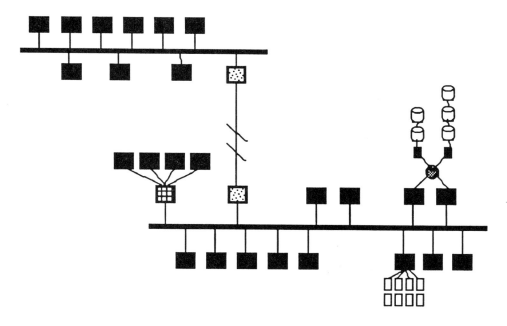

A Typical Ethernet

Ethernet is a Local Area Network (LAN) bus-oriented technology that is usually used to connect computers, printers, terminal concentrators (servers), and many other devices together. Ethernet itself is a hardware technology; it consists of a master cable and connection devices at each machine on the cable that allow the various devices to "converse" with each other. Additionally, software that knows how to access the Ethernet and also cooperates with machines connected to the cable is necessary for Ethernet to be truly useful.

Some History

Before Ethernet can be fully understood, it is necessary to learn a little about the history of Ethernet.

Ethernet got its beginnings from a network that was developed at the University of Hawaii in the early 1970's. Called ALOHA, the purpose of the network was to connect the main campus site in Oahu to seven other campuses located around four of the many islands that make up the State of Hawaii. The network was originally a ground-radio based terminal network that worked very much like separate radio stations communicating to a centralized radio station. What made ALOHA revolutionary and, therefore the "parent" of Ethernet, was the way that stations transmitted data on the network and, because of the mechanism involved, the simplicity of implementation and cost effectiveness.

Norman Abramson (a University of Hawaii professor) published a series of papers on the theory and applications of ALOHA (1969, 1970, 1973, 1977) that demonstrated a mechanism by which multiple stations on a network could use the same channel for multiple node communications. By utilizing a technique called contention, nodes would transmit data to the central facility in Oahu whenever they had data to send. If the frequency was not busy, the transmission was accepted and an acknowledgement was given to the station by the central hub node. If the node did not receive an acknowledgement (ACK) within a certain amount of time (200-1500ms), the remote station assumed that its packet had been collided with and would automatically resend the data. Through this mechanism, multiple nodes could communicate over the exact same frequencies in a simple and expeditious manner. Some of the ramifications are obvious. If there is no way to detect if another station is sending data, then it is logical to presume that there will be a good many collisions requiring retransmission. Another issue is the quality of signal: radio signals (this system uses FM for transmission) are notorious for being interfered with by weather, electrical interference, other signal interference, and many other related issued. Also, the more data and the more nodes that try to use the channel at the same time, the more retransmissions occur which can cause additional throughput delays. Based upon various tests that were performed on channel utilization vs. total resource availability, it has been estimated that "pure" ALOHA effectively uses 18% of the available resources. While this may seem inordinately inefficient, keep in mind that any station can send at any time. This means that the 18% is an average and if there is only one station transmitting at one time, 100% is used. It also illustrates one main problem with contention networks: the more data and nodes on the network contending for a resource, the more variable performance becomes.

In 1972, ALOHA was enhanced to provide some synchronization of access (this was called slotted ALOHA) and this effectively increased the effective usage of the channel resource to about 37%, but was still plagued with collisions over 26% of the time. To date, ALOHA has dramatically changed and has served as a model for packet broadcast systems in that it has expanded to satellite technology as well as local area networks.

But what does packet radio broadcasts have to do with Ethernet? Quite a lot. Ethernet derives its basic functionality (contention) from ALOHA and serves as a statement of what can happen from a good idea.

Formal Ethernet Development

The concept of Ethernet was originally developed at the now famous Xerox Palo Alto Research Center (PARC) as a method to allow the interconnection of office devices on a network that would allow high speed data transfer. The definitive paper on Ethernet was published in 1976 by R.M. Metcalf (now of 3COM fame) and D.R. Boggs. In the original implementation of Ethernet, a network that functioned at three mega-bits/ second (3Mbps) and allowed 100 connections was described. Additionally, the network demonstrated the capabilities of utilizing more than one device on the same cable transmission medium and allowing all devices on the cable to "contend" for the cable resource on a first-come first-served basis. Where Ethernet differs greatly from ALOHA is in collision detection. As we learned before, ALOHA allows anyone to transmit at any time. Ethernet does not. A station "listens" to the network to see if it is free. If it is, the station can send. If the cable is busy (a transmission is heard), the station waits until it can access and tries again. If two stations should happen to transmit at the same time, a state called a collision occurs and both stations back off, wait a random amount of time, and try again. Because of the randomness of arrival of traffic and the randomness of retransmissions, tests have shown that Ethernets, under a full load, can utilize, effectively, 90-95% of available resources.

Ethernet is not without limitations. Because of its contention nature, a finite number of nodes (systems) had to be imposed to insure that the resource would not become overly saturated. Additionally, a minimum packet size (64 bytes) and a maximum Ethernet segment length were imposed to allow the Ethernet stations the ability to guarantee the detection of collisions on the network. A maximum packet size was also imposed that allowed stations to know when a packet transmission should be complete, so as to help in the detection of errors on the network. Also, the Ethernet concept does not allow a guarantee of delivery of data. This means that data on the Ethernet, when delivered to the remote site, is not subject to sequence checks (making sure the packets arrive in the right order), missing packet retransmission requests, and other such necessities. These facilities are to be provided by on-system software (or hardware) facilities that cooperate with other nodes on a network.

Another issue of import is the length of the Ethernet cable. While we will be discussing more technical issues later, it is important to note that each segment of Ethernet (thickwire) has a length limitation of 500 meters. To extend the network requires specialized hardware, such as bridges and repeaters that can be costly and tricky to configure to stay within established guidelines. Ethernet, therefore, is a LOCAL area network, a network that is designed to provide communications in a building or, possibly, in a campus environment. It was not destined to be used in a wide-area mode where leased lines, and other types of connectivity (such as X.25 packet switching) have traditionally been used.

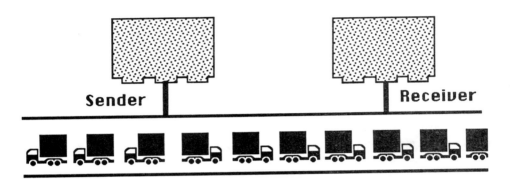

The easiest way to express the functionality of Ethernet is that it is a data "truck." Nodes wishing to communicate on the network allocate the "truck," put their data in the trailer section of the "truck," and send it out. The "truck" delivers the data to the remote station, but does not interpret, in any way, the contents in the trailer (data section of the packet). The end effect is that data is moved around very quickly as the overhead is minimal, the access fast, and the protocol is fairly efficient.

Following the initial testing of the 3Mbps Ethernet, performance analysis was done to assess the viability of such a network in the office environment. Statistics on an Ethernet showed an interesting distribution of resource utilization that is unlike other types of networks. Firstly, it is important to look at WHEN data arrives. In a 24-hour period, data arrives in "spurts" and cannot be depended upon to arrive in an even, flowing manner. Look at any business, and it is easily seen as to why. People do not all work 24 hours a day, computing does not happen in a constant manner, and data transfers happen at irregular intervals. So, statistics on Ethernet performance have to be looked upon with a calibrated eye. Because the nature of most office traffic is "bursty," it is logical to assume that the Ethernet will experience bursty usage. With this in mind, studies have shown that over a 24-hour day, the average load on test Ethernets (the 3Mbps kind) was usually less than 1%. If loading factors were looked upon at the worst times of the day, the following statistics on a 100 node 3Mbps Ethernet surfaced:

Worst second of the day:	40% saturation of the cable
Worst minute of the day:	15-20% saturation
Worst hour of the day:	3-5% saturation

What does all this mean? Simply that Ethernet performance is based directly on the arrival time of data and the amount of data being sent. Obviously, the nature of the data is directly related as well. File transfers, especially large ones, can tie up the resource and cause other file transfers to contend with each other. Lots of short, bursty traffic (such as control messages) cause a different kind of contention pattern to emerge. If very few nodes are communicating, fairly reasonable speeds can be expected and delivered. In short, the number of nodes, amount of traffic, and interarrival time distribution all factor in to Ethernet performance.

Over time, Xerox developed the Ethernet technology into a viable LAN technology that begins to provide the promised connectivity that would be necessary to solve office connectivity problems. With a new network technology also comes the need for software to control the technology and protocols such as the Xerox Network Services (XNS) protocol that were developed to provide enhanced connectivity services above the basic data transmission services offered by Ethernet.

The Vendor Consortium

As any good idea develops and spreads, so did Ethernet. Unfortunately, Xerox has been one the of the few companies that has not profited heavily from Ethernet product offerings. Through a consortium organized in the early 1980's, Xerox, Intel, and Digital Equipment Corporation published a vendor standard now known as the Ethernet Blue Book ("The Ethernet, Version 1.0," ACM Computer Comms Review, Vol 11, Number 2, July 1981, pp. 17 - 65). This book prescribed the methods in which Ethernets would be developed, implemented, and how the Ethernet hardware and data link services would work. This was further evolved and eventually produced a cooperative standard known Ethernet Version 2.0 in 1982.

What makes this consortium particularly interesting is that in many ways, Xerox and Digital are competitive companies in the office environment. Through the pool of multi-company talent, however, the basic 3Mbps Ethernet has been expanded, greatly, to the current 10Mbps version, and many of the restrictions on the original Ethernet standards have been modified or enhanced.

Standards and Ethernet

As the concept of LANs developed, many standardization organizations jumped on the proverbial bandwagon. Some began to organize standards for other types of network technologies that would serve the need of various types of business applications. LANs for offices, factories, process control environments, and many other applications began to appear. Such networks consisted of modified Ethernet concepts, token rings, token buses, twisted pair, fiber optic, and many other types of techniques and technologies. At the time the LANs were being proposed and explored, there was not an overwhelming demand from the potential customer base for such connectivity, and many networks and ideas simply faded away from lack of demand. Through it all, however, a select number of types of LANs became popular for various applications, and one standardization authority, the Institute for Electrical and Electronics Engineers (IEEE) formed a committee in February, 1980, to promote and provide LAN standards for use by industry (particularly office environments, initially). Called IEEE Project 802 (usually referred to in vendor circles as Committee 802), its charter is to provide LAN-oriented standards for consumers as well as related standards that allow interconnectivity between different Committee 802 standards.

IEEE Committee 802 generally develops standards that conform to the bottom three layers of the Open Systems Interconnect (OSI) model that was developed by the International Organization for Standardization (ISO) in 1978. The purpose of the OSI model was to provide an architectural model by which networks would be developed that would allow flexible enhancement and reconfiguration as well as interconnectivity with other compatible OSI- oriented networks. In the OSI model, layers 1 (Physical Layer) and 2 (Data Link Layer) are typically defined by the network technology being used. In the case of Ethernet, since it is predominantly hardware, it fulfills layers 1 and 2 of the OSI model quite nicely. Since the consortium of Xerox, Intel, and Digital had produced Ethernet, but not an acceptable domestic or international standard for the LAN technology, the IEEE formed subcommittee 802.3 and produced an IEEE standard for a technology very similar to the Ethernet specification. Due to its influence with domestic (U.S.) and international standardization authorities, IEEE standard 802.3 eventually became an ISO standard (IS 8802/3). Ethernet V2.0 (the Xerox/Intel/Digital standard) technological details were used as a basis for the IEEE 802.3 standard, but there were some fairly serious technical differences introduced in the IEEE standard that makes the two standards somewhat incompatible.

First, the physical characteristics of the prescribed cable are different. In the V2.0 standard, the Ethernet cable (thick wire) is prescribed to be a 50 ohm coaxial cable that is .395" in diameter. In the IEEE specification, the cable is still 50 ohms, but the diameter was increased to .405". On the surface, such a trivial amount of diameter difference does not seem like a great change. The IEEE, however, felt that the change was necessary for better electrical characteristics of the cable. On the negative side, however, it means that transceivers (the devices that attach to the Ethernet cable) that will connect to the cable must have a conductive spine that is long enough to reach the center conductor on the .405" diameter cable. Since the design of the transceiver includes a spine of appropriate length for the connection to the center conductor of the coaxial cable, V2.0 compliant transceivers' spines would not be long enough to reach the center conductor and make contact with same. This means that a V2.0 transceiver would not be able to connect, technically, to an IEEE compliant cable. In reality, many vendors have

provided a workaround by having upper transceiver assemblies that are capable of connecting to both V2.0 cables (.395") and 802.3 cables (.405" - PVC, .375" - Teflon).

Cable diameter is not the only thing that was changed between 802.3 and V2.0. When
transceivers are connected to the cable, there is usually no way to tell if the transceiver
is working or not unless data is actually transmitted to the network. In the V2.0 specification, a signal known as SQE (Signal Quality Error) is periodically generated by the
transceiver and read by the controller on the host system so that the controller knows
that the transceiver is, at least, alive. Over the years this has been known as the transceiver "heartbeat" and is used in the V2.0 specification as described. This presents a
problem in compatibility between the two standards. If a V2.0-compliant controller is
mated with a transceiver that is IEEE 802.3 compliant, the controller will think that
the transceiver is dead as 802.3-compliant transceivers do not necessarily generate a
heartbeat (SQE signal) unless a real signal quality error has occurred. Again, many vendors of transceivers have adapted to this issue by providing the capability of most transceivers to be switch-selectable between 802.3 and V2.0 by either setting jumpers
(wires) in the transceiver or a DIP switch accessible to the installer. It is important to
note that not all vendors have done this, so care should be exercised in the selection of
transceiver for a particular controller.

In the case of 802.3 compliant controllers, the need for SQE as a heartbeat is common.
Therefore, a V2.0 transceiver will usually work with most 802.3 controllers that plug
into host computers. Where the SQE as an actual error becomes a problem is with
802.3 compliant bridges and repeaters. In V2.0 compliant bridges and repeaters, the
bridge or repeater connected to a network segment expects SQE as a heartbeat. 802.3
compliant bridges and repeaters expect SQE to be an actual error. Therefore, transceivers
that generate SQE as a heartbeat may be used with all V2.0 controllers and most 802.3
compliant controllers. Transceivers that use SQE as an actual error signal are used with
802.3 compliant bridges and repeaters. Care should be exercised in the selection and
purchase of transceivers to make sure that the proper bridge and repeater requirements
are matched with the proper transceiver type.

A more important difference between the two standards is the issue of packet format on
the Ethernet or 802.3 (technically, 802.3 is NOT Ethernet, but most people call it
Ethernet nonetheless). On Ethernet V2.0 networks, controllers generate a packet format
as follows:

6 bytes	6 bytes	2 bytes	46-1500 bytes	4 bytes
Destination	Source	Type	Data	CRC-32

Prior to the destination address (48 bits), a 56-bit preamble and 8 bit start frame delimiter are transmitted. The preamble's function in life is to allow the physical signaling sublayer (PLS) circuitry the opportunity to reach its steady state. The start frame delimiter (SFD) is a bit sequence 10101011 that immediately follows the preamble and indicates that the frame (packet) being transmitted on the Ethernet is a valid frame.

Destination is the 48-bit Ethernet destination address that is usually encoded in ROM on each and every controller on an Ethernet. In reality, all 48 bits cannot be used for a particular node. The 48-bit field is actually broken down into three elements of bits that, together, make up the 48-bit address. The first element is called the LSB (Least Significant Bit) and will be either set to 0 if the address is an individual node address (singlecast message) or 1 if it is a group address (multicast or broadcast message). A group address is used on an Ethernet when a node wishes to send a message to more than one destination at a time. Who is a member of a particular group is up to the individual nodes; no one node tells other nodes what group they will be in. Each node must know this independently. The second element consists of setting the second bit in the 48-bit address to either 1 for a locally administered address or 0 for a globally (UPC) administered address. Locally administered addresses designate Ethernet addresses that are set up and identified by the local network control facility or personnel. Globally defined addresses are assigned by the current Ethernet address custodian, Xerox. At the time of this writing, there is a movement to change the address custodian to the IEEE, but this has not yet been decided. Global Ethernet addresses (UPCs) are assigned on a group basis to vendors who will be manufacturing Ethernet products that will be working on networks with more than one type of vendor hardware attached or in situations where the vendor of the hardware/software does not know what kind of Ethernet environment the developed products will exist in. The final element is the remaining 46 bits which are assigned on a node-by-node basis by the vendor of the product being used. These 46 bits usually designate a particular node or multicast address.

Ethernet addresses are usually installed in ROM by the manufacturer of the Ethernet controller and are usually represented in hexadecimal in a six-byte format such as 08-00-A0-01-FA-03. The source address is the sending machine's 48-bit address. The TYPE field is unique to V2.0 and stands for protocol type. In V2.0, a provision has been made to allow multiple protocols to exist on Ethernet at the same time. To facilitate the differentiation of protocols, Xerox prescribes the usage of the TYPE field for packets of certain protocols. Xerox functions as the custodian of protocol types and also as the custodian of the master list of Ethernet address ranges licensed to developers and manufacturers of Ethernet controllers. The DATA field the section of the Ethernet packet that would carry the data being transferred from one machine to another (usually some higher-level protocol such as Digital Data Communications Message Protocol (DDCMP), Local Area Transport (LAT), Xerox Network Services (XNS), Transmission Control Protocol/Internet Protocol (TCP/IP) or some other such protocol). A Cyclic Redundancy Check (CRC) is performed on the packet contents to insure that when the data gets to the destination node that all the data captured is correct.

A CRC-32 is computed as follows:

1. The destination, source, length/type, and data section are used to generate a number for function operations as follows:

$$G(x)=x^{32}+x^{26}+x^{23}+x^{22}+x^{16}+x^{12}+x^{11}+x^{10}+x^{8}+x^{7}+x^{5}+x^{4}+x^{2}+x^{1}$$

2. The first 32 bits of the frame are complemented

3. The n bits of the frame are then considered to be coefficients of a polynomial $M(x)$ of degree n-1. The first bit of the destination field corresponds to the $x^{(n-1)}$ term and the last bit of the data field corresponds to the x^0 term.

4. $M(x)$ is multiplied by x^{32} and divided by $G(x)$ producing a remainder $R(x)$ of degree < 31.

5. The coefficients of $R(x)$ are considered to be a 32-bit sequence

6. The bit sequence is complemented and the result is the CRC

By using a 32-bit CRC check, the chances of bad data being received and not detected is about 4.3 billion (2^{32-1}) to one.

In the case of IEEE 802.3, we see that the packet format is slightly different:

6 bytes	6 bytes	2 bytes	46-1500 bytes	4 bytes
Destination	Source	Length	Data	CRC-32

It is quite obvious that the TYPE field seen in the V2.0 specification is missing in the IEEE 802.3 specification. By non-inclusion of the TYPE field, compatibility cannot be maintained among the two standards and there is no workaround. In fact, the same bit locations used for the TYPE field in the V2.0 specification are used for a field that contains the length of the data. Another anomaly is the option of using 48-bit or 16-bit node addresses in the IEEE specification. Because of this particular anomaly, when the 16-bit addressing scheme is employed, only IEEE compliant nodes may communicate with each other. Another anomaly is the inclusion of IEEE 802.2 Logical Link Control (LLC) information in the begining of the DATA section on 802.3 frames. LLC information allows the remote (desitnation) node to know what entity on the source node sent the packet. It also allows for identity of the type of 802.3 frame as there are different types (in accordance with IEEE 802.2). Therefore, when considering network technologies, IEEE 802.3 and Ethernet V2.0 are different in some fairly obvious ways (as illustrated) and in some not-so-obvious ways (there are also some additional subtle but not so critical differences).

There still exists a third format for the packet. A specialized format used for control messages is provided for in the 802.2 network management specification and is supported by vendors who provide the capability to produce Class I (control) packet types. The previously described 802.3 packet type is also known as a Class II packet or user-defined packet.

Ethernet and 802.3 are different enough as to be incompatible. How the incompatibility occurred is due to political as well as technical issues involved that are best left to historians and analysts. For our purposes, it suffices to say that caution MUST be exercised when considering Ethernet or 802.3 and the fact remains that they are incompatible. If you are considering usage of Ethernet technology, make sure that all cooperating nodes either "speak" V2.0 format or 802.3 format. In some instances, some vendors have been clever enough to implement logic in their controllers that understand both formats, but these controllers are not common and must still be carefully scrutinized before selection and use.

One thing to point out is the *trend for most vendors to support the IEEE 802.3 version rather than Ethernet V2.0*. The reason for this is fairly straightforward. With the impending implementation of a complete OSI-compliant network (with OSI-prescribed protocols at each layer of the architecture), it is important for vendors developing OSI-compliant networks to adhere to ISO standards for same. Since IEEE 802.3 is an ISO standard as well as being prescribed for access at layers 1 and 2 of the OSI model, it is obvious that if a vendor wants to get the most mileage from its development effort, it should develop software and hardware around the 802.3 standard when implementing Ethernet technology. There is nothing intrinsically wrong with the V2.0 standard other than it is a vendor standard only and does not comply with the prescribed ISO standard for the Ethernet-like network.

For the purposes of discussion in the rest of this book, we will consider 802.3 and V2.0 to both be Ethernet, but, in reality, 802.3 is technically NOT Ethernet whereas V2.0 is.

Why Ethernet is Called Ethernet.

By the way, while we're on the subject of history, you are probably wondering why Ethernet is called "Ethernet." When Ethernet was being proposed years ago, it was billed as the ultimate network that would tie in everything in the office or other such environment. It derives its name from the old electromagnetic theoretical substance termed "luminiferous ether" (not the stuff used to knock-out patients in days of yore), a matter that was thought to be the universal element that bound together the entire universe and all associated parts. An "ether" net would be, therefore, a network that would effectively bind together all components located on the net.

Where are Ethernets Used?

Ethernet history goes back a way, but actual usage of Ethernets in a commercial way has only recently become a reality. For quite a while, the necessary components to construct and provide viable and functional Ethernet products have either been unavailable due to technological reasons or due to excessive cost factors. In the last few years, however, VLSI has provided suitable technological and cost effective solutions to make Ethernet product production a viable and profitable venture for network vendors.

Ethernet has a traditional and historic role in the office place. By installing Ethernet in an office or building environment, a variety of products and services may be offered to computing "clients." Services such as shared printers, shared disks and files, terminal distribution systems, and many other services are available, today, as products on Ethernets. Some vendors are currently experimenting with still video on Ethernets and high-resolution graphics access. Other vendors have provided mechanisms by which disk-less workstations may access common disk structures located on remote systems as if the disks were directly connected to the system using the disk resource.

Ethernets are also seen in industrial and lab networks as well. Long hailed for its speed and ease of installation and use, Ethernets are also known for their reliability and tolerance of potential interference from sources such as electrical motors, radio frequency emissions, and many other sources of distortion. Ethernets are seen in robotics applications, factory automation (controlling radio-controlled vehicles and automated assembly lines), process control (controlling chemical reactions, power plants, furnace systems, etc...), and many other non-office applications where a high-speed, reliable network is necessary.

When is an Ethernet Appropriate for Your Needs

Choosing whether or not an Ethernet is appropriate or not for your network solution requires some thought and consideration. Ask yourself the following questions when considering Ethernet as a solution. It is important to note that these questions are centered around Ethernet limitations and capabilities that will be addressed in this book, so you will discover the reasons for the questions as you proceed through the book:

o Are your farthest nodes more than 500 meters apart?
  a) If YES, are they more than 37 miles apart?

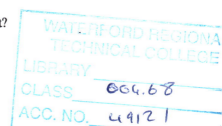

21

o Do you have a need to share resources amongst multiple
   machines?
o Are you expecting a rapid growth curve in network nodes?
o Are you in a high network traffic environment?
o Is most of your network traffic destined for one main system?
o Is your main network application one that requires a
   predictable and reliable network response time?
o Will you or your staff be installing most network
   connections?
o Do you have the need to connect to existing networks in your
   company?
o Is high-availability of the network a critical issue?
o Will you be connecting various types of systems and devices?
o Is network maintenance an issue?

These questions are to provide you thought-provoking stimulus about the things that
must be considered when contemplating an Ethernet for your networking needs. In the
remainder of this book, we will discover in depth how Ethernet technology works,
planning, installation, management, maintenance, enhancements, and other related issues necessary in the consideration and implementation of Ethernet networks.

Chapter Summary

Not all "Ethernets" are **Ethernet**. There can be substantial differences between implementations as evidenced by the differences between the DEC/Intel/Xerox Ethernet and
the IEEE 802.3 implementation. While both provide CSMA/CD and extremely similar
functionality, the protocol implementations and physical characteristics are different
enough to cause implementation problems.

Chapter Three

Ethernet Technological Details

The ideas I stand for are not mine. I borrowed them from Socrates. I swiped them from Chesterfield. I stole them from Jesus. And I put them in a book. If you don't like their rules, whose would you use?

Dale Carnegie

Introduction

As with any product, Ethernet has a prescribed list of capabilities and limitations. In this chapter, we will explore how Ethernet works and some issues involved in its implementation.

Basic Components

Ethernet, as previously described, is a Local Area Network (LAN) technology that is used to connect various computers or "smart" devices together, typically (but not exclusively) in an office environment. Ethernets come in various "flavors" such as baseband and broadband and may run on a variety of different media such as coax, twisted pair, and fiber.

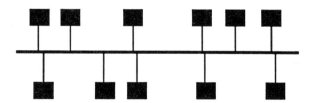

An Ethernet is configured in a "bus" topology. This means that there is a backbone (main) cable on which communicating systems and peripherals are attached (the networking term is "tapped"). Taps may be intrusive (the cable must be cut for the tap to be included) or non-intrusive (the cable is drilled and a tap added without disturbing the integrity or operation of the network). By definition, a baseband Ethernet (the most common) is tapped non-intrusively and broadband Ethernets usually require intrusive taps for connecting nodes. Most Ethernets only allow 100 taps per master segment of thickwire coaxial cable.

Data Encoding

Data is transmitted on Ethernet in a manner known as Manchester encoding. Manchester encoding is a technique used to encode transmitted data on the cable to insure that the end of transmission (Carrier-Sense failure) is properly detected. As you are probably already aware, digital data is transmitted by a series of on-off electrical pulses. When the pulse is "on," the line is said to be at a high level. Where there is no pulse during the transmission ("off" state), the line is said to be in a low state.

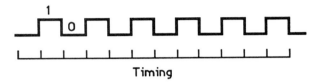

A Typical Digital Transmission

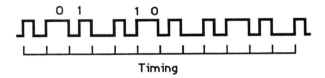

A Manchester Encoded Digital Transmission

Manchester encoding differs from a standard digital transmission in that instead of a high being a "1" and a low being a "0," a timing interval is used to measure high-to-low transitions and the transmissions of 1's and 0's differs slightly. Instead of the timed transmission period being "all high" or "all low" for either a 1 or a 0, a state transition is encoded into the transformation. A 1 is sent as a half-time-period low followed by a half-time-period high. Conversely, a 0 is sent as a half-time-period high followed by a half-time-period low. Because of this, the end of the last bit being sent is easily determined immediately following the transmission of the last bit (usually this takes about 160ns).

Baseband Ethernet

Baseband Ethernet is an implementation of Ethernet where the entire bandwidth of a particular backbone cable is used for nothing except Ethernet communications. If a co-axial cable had, say, a bandwidth of 500MHz, the entire 500MHz would be used to send Ethernet traffic. A baseband Ethernet also is terminated at both ends with 50ohm terminators and is grounded **ON ONE END ONLY** to earth or building ground, depending upon ground potential hazard (always have a licensed master electrician ground the cable to prevent shock hazard; not a lot of voltage appears, but there can be a high number of amps). Another feature: baseband allows non-intrusive tapping. The thickwire coaxial cable is typically pre-marked every two and one-half meters where taps will be placed (on thickwire Ethernet cables taps are placed 2.5 meters apart and are designated by a black ring around the cable; thinwire is tapped at 2.5 meter intervals, but the RG58 cable is usually not marked).

Baseband Ethernet can run on various types of media, each of which imposes restrictions on how close nodes can be tapped from each other and on total cable distances for a segment. Thickwire coax has a distance limitation of 500 meters, whereas thinwire coax (RG58R/U) has limitations anywhere from 189 meters to 1000 meters (although 189 is most common and in the 802.3 standard) depending upon the vendor of the transceivers and the network controllers. Twisted pair Ethernets (10Mbps type) run from 20 meters up to 100 meters (currently) and fiber optic Ethernets have length restrictions anywhere from 30 meters to 5000 meters (at this time). The various length restrictions have to do with specific media propagation delays and noise factors on each type of cable plus logic restrictions in the controllers and transceivers.

While all types of media use the baseband method of transmitting data on the cable, not all cables can be directly connected to each other. Connection of a fiber to a thinwire cannot be done through a barrel connector; rather a special type of repeater must be used. In some situations, however, thinwire can be connected via barrel connector to a thickwire baseband Ethernet, but the length restrictions on the overall segment vary depending upon how much of the cable is thickwire and how much is thinwire. If you are considering taking such an approach, use the following formula to calculate the total cable length:

$$(3.28 * \text{Thinwire length}) + \text{Thickwire length} < 500 \text{ meters}$$

As an example, if the thinwire section were 100 meters in length and the thickwire 50 meters in length, the total length, physically, of the cable would be 150 meters. However, electrically the cable would appear as a 378 meter Ethernet. So, thinwire can be connected to thickwire, but you must compensate for the differences in signal (thinwire has a higher signal loss problem) strength and noise factors.

If baseband segments from differing kinds of media are connected, it is usually recommended that a repeater or a bridge be used (explained in Chapter Four).

Broadband Ethernet

Broadband implementations of Ethernet are markedly different than the baseband implementations. In the case of broadband, taps must be carefully placed as the network is basically a private cable TV network. Broadband networks have an advantage over baseband networks in that they may be considerably larger than a baseband network. Baseband networks typically are 500 meters per segment total length and the entire network may not exceed 2.5km total distance. Broadband networks allow the network to extend, easily, to lengths up to 37-50 miles. Adding on broadband segments is fairly easy as well: broadband networks may "T" off of the master backbone without using repeaters or bridges, allowing for very flexible network configurations. On the down side, a broadband network is like running your own private TV station. Its base transmission method is analog and uses a technique called Frequency Division Multiplexing (FDM) to split up the 500Mhz or so bandwidth in the cable (some cables have a much higher bandwidth; 500MHz is being used as an example) into usable sub-channels for Ethernet, voice, video, and other signals. Since the network allows multiple channels, it is quite possible to run multiple Ethernets on the same physical medium by running the different Ethernets on different channels in the spectrum.

1010101110101001110101 01

Baseband

101010101110100101001110011010100110100111001	Freq. A
101010101110100101001110011010100110100111001	Freq. B
101010101110100101001110011010100110100111001	Freq. C

Broadband

An Ethernet on a broadband typically requires about 12-18MHz per data channel, and two data channels are required for each Ethernet on the broadband. As a basis for comparison, consider that a typical NTSC-encoded color television signal takes about 6MHz of bandwidth. Since Ethernet traffic is digital data, not an analog signal, it requires more bandwidth per channel. Additionally, most broadbands are unidirectional in nature. This means that when data is transmitted on the network, the propagation is in a single direction, typically towards the head-end amplifier (a required item on a broadband Ethernet). For the Ethernet to function properly, a send channel and a receive channel are required in the broadband environment, effectively utilizing a minimum of 24-36MHz of bandwidth, not counting frequency separation from other signals on the cable.

For a more thorough treatment of the subject of broadband Ethernet, I suggest reading Edward Cooper's book on the subject (see the Recommended Reading List at the back of this book). It is well written and explains the technology well.

Transceivers & Ethernet Cable

Tapping a cable is obviously not sufficient to allow communications; an electrical interface of some kind is required to be able to connect to the cable. In the case of Ethernet, such an interface is called a transceiver. Transceivers come in many shapes and sizes (as well as price ranges), but they all provide one basic function: allow a system to communicate with the cable.

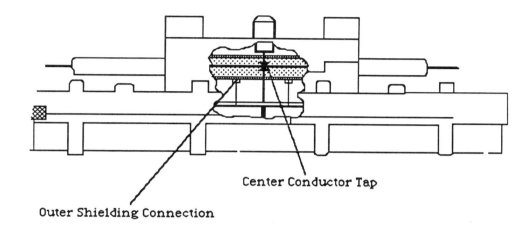

Center Conductor Tap

Outer Shielding Connection

Cutaway View of a Transceiver

A transceiver is so named because it transmits and receives simultaneously. What this translates to is that when a system is sending information on to the Ethernet cable, the transceiver's transmitting circuitry is sending the bits of data while the transceiver's receiving circuitry is listening to the data that is being sent. If the transceiver detects that the data that is being sent by the transmitting side of the transceiver is the same as that being received by the receiver side, all is well. If, however, the two sides do not match, the transceiver presumes that a collision has happened and notified the controller card on the host system. A transceiver is fairly dumb: it sends data, receives data, and notifies the host controller if a collision situation has occurred. In the case of a V2.0 Ethernet, the transceiver also asserts SQE - Signal Quality Error (explained later) periodically, letting the controller know that it is alive. If your controller is of the 802.3 persuasion, you will need a transceiver that does not use the SQE signal or one that is switch selectable between the two.

Some vendors, such as Digital Equipment Corporation (DEC), have developed specialized boxes that allow more than one system to connect to a single transceiver tap. The

DEC Digital Ethernet Local Network Interconnect (DELNI) box allows up to eight systems to connect to the box and a single Ethernet transceiver taps the eight systems on to the main Ethernet cable. A side effect of the DELNI is the ability for the DELNI to function standalone and emulate an eight-tap Ethernet cable. In cases where the systems are no more than 50 meters away from the DELNI or there are no more than eight co-located systems that need to be on an Ethernet, the DELNI is more cost-effective than a chunk of Ethernet cable and eight transceivers. Not to mention more convenient. On the down side, the DELNI does have its own power supply, so if it fails, for whatever reason, up to eight nodes may not be able to access the network. Other vendors make DELNI-like boxes, so the DEC box is by no means unique to DEC. Another issue is that if a transceiver compensator box, such as the DELNI, is connected to the Ethernet segment, the overall cable length may need to be examined. An 8-connection transceiver compensator is the equivalent of 20 meters of cable with eight connections (taps). This can mean that the backbone cable may need to be reduced in total length to compensate for the attached transceiver compensators. Check with the Ethernet vendor to insure that the network will still be compliant after connection of such compensators, especially on very long segments (those that approach the 500 meter length restriction). Be careful, however. Such boxes react to the host(s) exactly like a transceiver, so make sure that the box that you put in place emulates either V2.0 or 802.3 as required by your controller on the system. If you install the wrong kind of box, the connection from your system to the Ethernet may not work properly.

Transceiver Cables

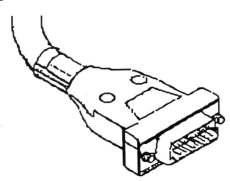

From the transceiver a 15-pin cable is run to a cable-mounting bracket (called the bulkhead assembly) in the back of a system or peripheral. This is aptly enough called the transceiver cable. Transceiver cables come in a variety of lengths, but more vendors do not allow a transceiver cable to exceed 50 meters in total length and some require the transceiver cable to be somewhat shorter. The transceiver cable does more than provide the wiring for the data transfer and handshakes between the controller and the transceiver. Because the transceiver usually does not have a power supply of its own, the transceiver cable also has a wire (one of the 15 pins) that supplies power from the host system controller to the transceiver. A transceiver cable has to be carefully selected as different transceiver and controller makers have different ways to connect the cable to the transceiver or to the system bulkhead assembly. Some vendors use a new sliding-lock system as specified in the IEEE 802.3 specification; others opt for the traditional brass screw approach. Both connectors work fine, but only with the proper destination fitting. Make sure that the connectors selected will work with the cables selected. If you are going to have your own transceiver cables custom made (many companies do), insure that the proper connectors are selected.

Host System Interfaces (Controllers)

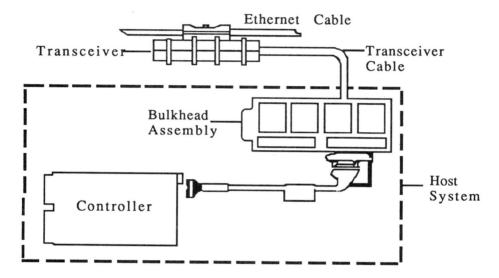

To connect the host system properly to the transceiver assembly, a controller board or circuitry must be provided on the host system. Such controllers are usually add-on cards that system vendors provide for an additional cost. Different systems have different connectivity requirements, so it is very important to get a controller that matches the system hardware that is being used and also a controller that will be able to properly communicate with the networking software that will be used on the host system.

Controllers typically consist of a minimum of three separate sets of functional components: the Ethernet interface circuitry, on-board processor, microcode and ROM/RAM, and a host system bus interface. The Ethernet interface circuitry is typically provided by one of the standard chipsets from Intel, AMD, or other such manufacturer of chip subsystems. The processor, microcode, and RAM/ROM varies from vendor to vendor due to the different requirements as defined by the customer base and the functions that the Ethernet controller will provide. For instance, some controllers such as the Excelan card allow TCP/IP protocol functionality to be provided in the controller in addition to the ability to access Ethernet. While this is a useful feature, the card may be worthless if the main communications goal is to have Ethernet access as well as utilize other non-TCP communications packages. Why? No, there is nothing wrong with the Excelan card - as a matter of fact, it is a fine controller. The problem is that some communications architectures expect a cooperating Ethernet controller to react in certain mysterious ways that the Excelan card does not provide.

Different controllers obviously have different capabilities. Oddly enough, even different controllers from the same hardware vendor for the exact same host system may have different capabilities. As an example, consider the DEUNA and DELUA controllers from DEC. Both controllers allow connectivity to an Ethernet on a DEC UNIBUS-based system (PDP-11 or VAX). The DEUNA is an older controller, but works quite well. The DELUA is newer, however, and makes use of advanced technology Ethernet chips as well as additional microcode and other capabilities which allow it to run at twice the speed of the DEUNA plus support some extensions to Ethernet that are useful to certain DEC communications products. Therefore, when selecting Ethernet controllers to satisfy a communications need, consider the following:

o Will the controller support the selected software environment?
o Is the controller access speed well matched to system capabilities?
o Is there a compatible transceiver for the controller?
o Does the controller have special host system requirements?
o Is the controller supported by the host system as a "native" controller?
o Are the levels of buffering in the controller adequate for the expected load factors?
o What is the MTBF and MTTR factors for the controller?
o Does the controller support V2.0 or IEEE 802.3 or both?
o Is there host interface (drivers) software for the controller?
o Is the controller customer configurable?
o Is the controller programmable by the customer?
o Will the controller support a multiple-protocol environment?
o Will the controller experience problems if other Ethernet controllers are on the same system?
o What software packages are available for the controller and will they work concurrently on the controller and host system?

Host Software

While technically not a part of an Ethernet, the host software is extremely important to Ethernet, as an Ethernet is fairly worthless without it. As previously discussed, Ethernet is a "data mover." As an analogy, the phone system carries voice. It does not provide for retransmission of spoken words if a burst of static is encountered or if the connection is lost. Ethernet works the same way. As a datagram service, Ethernet simply sends data on the network. If the packet arrives at the proper destination in one piece, great. If not, that's OK - there's plenty more when the last packet came from. The data that gets moved is whatever the host system decides to send or allows receipt of. In the case of Ethernet, the Ethernet packet protocol is fairly simple and well defined. How the host gets to the network is defined by the controller and associated interface software. Typically, a company would select a particular network architecture or technology approach that satisfies a particular requirement or group of requirements. This network technology would usually provide the connectivity required by utilizing a protocol or series of protocols over the Ethernet (the protocols used would be encapsulated in the DATA segment of the Ethernet packet). It is up to the host software to sort out the destination for various protocols used over Ethernet as the Ethernet definition does not provide for any such screening or assistance. Since not all host software packages are capable of accepting multiple protocols or multiple types of Ethernet controllers, care must be exercised in the selection and utilization of protocols on the Ethernet.

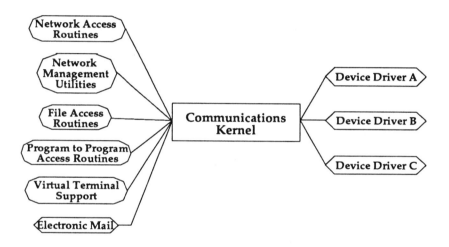

Host software packages range from terminal services packages to full-function network packages (program-to-program, file transfer, remote file access, virtual terminal support, etc.). In all cases, many packages expect to use either a particular Ethernet controller type or a class of Ethernet controllers on particular machine architectures. Some standalone, dedicated systems (such as terminal server systems) use a particular protocol that may not be modified and will only work with a fairly rigidly defined set of devices or services.

Types of Protocols

Another issue in the selection of host software on Ethernets is the problem of base software architectural issues. Ethernet, properly configured, is a fairly stable and reliable network. As a result, communications architectures designed for unstable network technologies (such as dial-up lines) will typically incur overhead that is counterproductive in a LAN environment. As such, most host communications software architectures usually fall into one of two categories:

1. **Connection-oriented protocol.** In this type of communications architecture, cooperating nodes on a network constantly send initialization (init) and "HELLO" messages to insure that the remote system is available and reachable. The init and HELLO messages are essential on unstable links and help guarantee that the links are available when required. This type of communications method is also referred to as "circuit-oriented."

2. **Connectionless-oriented protocol.** This type of protocol handling, while not unique to LANs, is ideally suited for LANs as it makes best use of available resources. Typically, a connectionless-oriented protocol will send messages only when there is data or messages to send. If initialization or "HELLO" messages are required, they are only sent if the remote node does not properly acknowledge message or control sequences or when a node is initially activating. Network technologies that take advantage of this type of mechanism incur less host overhead and also less control traffic on the network. This type of communications method is sometimes called "socket oriented."

Which one is better than the other is difficult to say as each provides a unique method of connection mechanism. In the LAN environment, however, traditional communications protocols from some network architectures may not be well suited for usage of Ethernet as a communications medium, so care should be exercised in the selection process. Check out vendor claims carefully and insist on examining running nodes and talking to other customers about their experiences with the selected architecture.

By and large, however, connection-less protocols are better suited for LAN technologies such as Ethernet. Since connection-oriented network technologies usually require a good deal of synchronization, the overhead on the network can be extreme, especially if there is signal loss or errors on the line. Connection-less protocols help reduce overall traffic load and rely on a semi-reliable communications medium, such as Ethernet.

How does Ethernet Work?

Now that we have discussed the basic components of Ethernet, let's discuss how Ethernet actually works.

CSMA/CD

The basis of Ethernet operation is an access method called Carrier Sense Multiple Access with Collision Detection, also known as CSMA/CD. Don't let the long title intimidate you, as the mechanism involved is fairly simple.

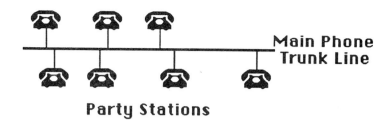

Main Phone Trunk Line

Party Stations

CSMA/CD is easy to understand if you imagine Ethernet as an old-style telephone party line. The way that party lines work is simple: one phone line is shared by many phones installed in various homes or businesses. If someone wants to use the line, the phone is lifted from the receiver ("off-hook" in telephony terms), the customer listens to make sure no one else is talking and, if no one else is speaking, the customer may then place a call or speak. Calls to a particular phone on a party line were placed by ringing all phones on the party line in a particular pattern (such as two short rings and one long ring might be the Smiths; one long ring and two short rings might be Jones family, etc.). If a customer is already talking, all other stations politely wait until the line is clear (no one is speaking). If two people speak at the same time, both will typically stop and wait a random amount of time before trying again (after all, we're presuming that everyone on the party line is polite). Another way to look at it is a polite conversation between a group of people at a cocktail party. Only one person at a time speaks and all others listen and hear all that is being spoken. If two people start to speak at the same time, both will usually back-off, wait a random amount of time, and try again.

In the case of Ethernet, the above paragraph pretty accurately describes what happens. Nodes (systems) on the network all connect to the master cable and wait until data is to be sent. When any data is sent on the network, all nodes "hear" all data sent. By examining the first 48 bits in each message transmitted, nodes may determine if the message is destined for itself or another node. If the message is for another node, it is usually ignored. If the message is addressed to the listening node, the message is copied into the controller in its entirety and passed up to the host system. If a node wishes to transmit data to another node on the network, the originating node listens to see if the line is quiet (this is called sensing for carrier). If the network is quiet, the originating node begins to transmit its data. As it transmits its data, it also immediately receives the same data and compares it with the transmitted data. If the transmitted data matches the received data, the data is being successfully transmitted.

Collisions and Detection

If the data received does not match the transmitted data, it is logical to assume that some sort of distortion (collision) has occurred either by some other node sending data

33

at the same time or some other anomaly such as noise or a bad transceiver babbling (sending out spurious noise or trash) on the line. If the transceiver detects a collision, it notifies the controller and the controller stops sending the data. To guarantee that any other nodes sending data hear the collision, the controller sends a burst of noise on the line (also called a "jam"). The controller then generates a random number that dictates how long the controller will wait before attempting to re-send the message. Once the random time interval has elapsed, the controller again listens to see if the line is clear. If so, the transceiver begins to send and listen to the sent information to insure that it is correct. If the message is transmitted in its entirety and the information received in the transceiver matches the information sent by the transceiver, the packet is judged by the controller as having been successfully sent and the controller either readies another packet for transmission or listens for data on the network. In the case of the packet being collided with on the re-transmission attempt, the controller takes a slightly different approach. Noise is sent just like the first collision occurrence, but a random number is not generated as before. Rather, the controller doubles the previously generated random number and waits the prescribed time before attempting retransmission. If further collisions occur, the doubling operation will continue up to a prescribed number of times (usually 16) after which the controller will usually dump the packet and send an error message up to the host system notifying it of the "multiple collision" occurrence.

What insures that Ethernet controllers and transceivers accurately detect collisions when they occur is the usage of a minimum Ethernet packet size (64 bytes) and a maximum Ethernet cable segment length and propagation time. Through these methods, used together, by the time the last bit of the last byte of information is transmitted the originating node is guaranteed of detecting a collision condition between its transmission operation and any other attempt at transmission on the network at the same time.

The Ethernet Packet

Destination	Source	Type	Data	CRC-32

Ethernet V2.0 Packet Format

Destination	Source	Length	Data	CRC-32

IEEE 802.3 Packet Format

As we have discussed in Chapter Two, Ethernet packets are arranged in two different formats: V2.0 and 802.3.

The format of the packet is rigid and may not be altered except as defined by the standard (in the 802.3 standard, 2-byte addresses may be allowed). Let's examine each field.

Destination Address

The destination address is fairly obvious: who is supposed to receive the packet that is being sent. What is not so obvious is that there are three types of destination addresses:

1. **Singlecast address.** In this situation, the destination address field contains one 6 byte (48-bit) address that matches one and only one node.

2. **Multicast address.** This destination address "looks" like it is destined to only one node and is still a 6-byte address, but it is a special address that various nodes may know about and receive as if though the packet was addressed in a singlecast way to the receiving node. An example of when multicast messages are sent is the situation of downline system loading. The system requesting the load sends out a message destined to all nodes on the network segment that know how to load remote systems. Which systems these are is not known to the load requestor; all it has to do is send the message to the generic "loader" address. If there is a node on the network that knows how to satisfy the request, the load is performed.

3. **Broadcast address.** The broadcast address, FF-FF-FF-FF-FF-FF is the only one on the entire network. When data is sent to the broadcast address, every node on the entire network will receive and accept the packet. The problem is obvious: if every node, regardless of vendor and software, receives the packet, there will be a lot of nodes that will reject the packet as unintelligible. For this reason, the broadcast address is usually not used on Ethernets by most communications software vendors. Do not get broadcast addresses confused with the broadcast "nature" of Ethernet. Because of the broadcast nature of Ethernet, all packets are seen by all nodes, but not all packets will be accepted or interpreted by all nodes. If a message is sent to the broadcast address, all nodes will scan and accept the packet.

Typically, the destination address is the 48-bit address of the destination controller. As you will recall, the 48-bit addresses on Ethernet are all encoded in ROM in the controllers that are sold by controller vendors. How other nodes learn about the 48-bit addresses is up to the networking architecture (software) being used over the Ethernet. Some architectures send the address as part of the node initialization cycle. Other communications programs periodically broadcast the address and other node information as a multicast packet. In any case, for a node to be reached, the originating node must know its destination address.

Special Types of Node Addresses

Some vendors, however, also use "virtual" destination (and source) node addresses. An example is the DECnet product as it applies to Ethernet. DEC had to make a decision to support Ethernet some time back. It also made the strategic decision to support 48-bit addressing on Ethernet. While this seems like a reasonable expectation, in the case of DEC is can also cause problems. Since Ethernet expects, usually, 48-bit node addresses, DEC had to figure out a way to get its 16-bit DECnet node addresses to function properly in the 48-bit Ethernet address environment. While the obvious answer is to expand the size of DECnet node addresses, this is a difficult and tedious thing to do as DECnet runs on a variety of machine architectures and is made up of a variety of implementations. Some systems would not be able to support 48-bit addressing without some very substantial upgrades to the software and controller microcode. As a result, the problem of getting DECnet on all operating systems to work properly with Ethernet was a profound one indeed.

Instead of a massive re-code operation, DEC adopted a clever tack. By allocating a secondary range of addresses for Ethernet from Xerox, DEC stripped off the lower 16-bits from a range of the allocated addresses to allow 16-bit addresses to be used by adding on a 32-bit adder. Through the use of a simple algorithm, DECnet 16-bit node addresses (defined in software on the host) are converted to 48-bit "virtual" addresses. For example, if a node's address were 20.250 (20 = DECnet area number and 250 = node address in the area), this address is converted to a 16-bit hexadecimal number as follows:

$$(20 * 1024) + 250 = 20710 = 50E6 \text{ (hex)}$$

DEC utilizes the upper 32-bit stream of AA-00-04-00 as the 32-bit adder to the created 16-bit node address from DECnet. By adding the generated address to the 32-bit adder, a 48-bit node address is created:

$$AA\text{-}00\text{-}04\text{-}00\text{-}E6\text{-}50 = \text{DECnet node } 20.250$$

You will notice that the 50 and E6 have been reversed. This is due to the method in which DEC systems load data into storage or registers (low order byte first). In any case, now the 16-bit DECnet address is a full 48-bit Ethernet address and readily usable in the Ethernet environment. A side benefit is that controllers that know about the upper 32-bit adder can immediately ascertain if they are talking to a DECnet node or not based upon the first 32-bits of the address.

Source Addresses

After the explanation above, the source address should be pretty obvious: it is the address of the originating node. Source addresses are usually the ROM encoded address and are NEVER a multicast or broadcast address. In some cases, such as DECnet, the source address may be a virtual address created by the controller or software to allow connectivity to other nodes.

Data Section

The data section is the simplest of all sections in the packet format. The DATA section may contain practically anything in any format. Since Ethernet does not interpret the DATA section (except for the first 16-bits, which is either protocol type or the length of the data section), anything may be located in the section depending upon what the communications architecture wishes to send. In any case, the data section must be a minimum length of 46 bytes (even if there is only one byte to send, it MUST be at least 46 bytes in size) and may be as large as 1500 bytes. Typically, the DATA section would contain the protocol packet used by the host software communications architecture (such as DDCMP, MOP, LAT, XNS, TCP/IP, etc...).

Cyclic Redundancy Check (CRC)

The purpose of a cyclic redundancy check (CRC) is to insure that the data delivered to the remote is still accurate and has not suffered a bit error of some kind, which would render the data useless and cause other important problems. Ethernet prescribes the use of a CRC-32, which is a 32-bit cyclic redundancy check. A CRC is nothing more extravagant than long division based upon a certain bit string or size of bit string. After the division is completed, the appropriate number of levels (32 in the case of CRC-32), the remainder is used as the checksum. When a packet is received, the checksum is "reverse divided" and matched to the supposed original. If there is a match, the packet is intact. If there is not a match, the packet is erroneous and discarded. The number of bits in the CRC are important - the more bits, the less the chance of an error getting through undetected. For instance, a 32-bit CRC implies that the chances of a bit error getting through the error check undetected are about 4.3 billion to one. If the check were 16 bits, the chances drop to 65536 to one.

Obviously the resolution of the CRC requires additional computational cycles on the system or in the controller to provide fast CRC's. Some vendors have designed chips to perform CRC's in the controller hardware to speed up the processing of incoming and outgoing packets. It should be noted that in addition to the required CRC-32 on the Ethernet packet format, frequently upper layers of software also provide CRC's for packet consistency.

Chapter Summary

While Ethernet comes in various configurations and utilizes various types of media, the same basics of data transmission, error detection, and control apply to most popular implementations. Ethernet can be used in a wide variety of applications from classic network applications to newer uses, such as terminal distribution subsystems.

In all cases, Ethernet is nothing more than a data truck facility. Upper layers of software are required for Ethernet to be a truly useful network technology. Such layers provide the necessary functions for a network to be truly useful in network applications.

Chapter Four

Repeaters, Bridges and Servers

I tell thee, be not rash; a golden bridge is for a flying enemy.
Lord Byron

Introduction

Many times the restrictions on length of Ethernet segments becomes a problem. With a 500-meter-segment-length restriction on baseband networks (the least expensive of configurations and, therefore, the most popular), large, multi-story buildings and factory environments have trouble implementing Ethernet. With the use of repeaters and bridges, however, multiple 500-meter segments can be connected together.

Another valuable feature of using repeaters and bridges is that segments of Ethernet are now connected together (effectively "looking" like one large Ethernet), but separate for connectivity purposes. Should a segment experience a failure, it does not disable the entire network, as a single segment would. This feature is usually referred to as segment isolation.

Once the segments are connected, there are many times that sharable devices are required. Also, vendors have implemented small diskless systems that provide terminal connectivity to remote systems on an Ethernet.

In this chapter we shall explore what these various connection technologies are and how they fit in to the overall Ethernet scheme of things.

I Repeat, You Repeat, He, She, It Repeats!

One of the oldest technologies used to connect Ethernet segments together has been a device called a repeater. A repeater typically consists of some sort of microprocessor (such as a MC68000), ROM code, and the ability to connect to transceivers on two separate Ethernet segments. Repeaters are standalone units (they need no master or load host) and basically perform the function of repeating everything that is heard on one segment on to the other segment and vice-versa. This task seems pretty easy and, for the most part, it is except that such work has to be done in a BIG hurry if the network is not to suffer a performance degradation.

Repeater Configurations

Repeaters are usually configured in one of two methods: local or remote.

In the local configuration, a repeater box is connected, directly, between two Ethernet segments. The connection on each segment is a transceiver and as far as the Ethernets themselves are concerned, the repeater is simply another node tapped in. The repeater, however, knows different.

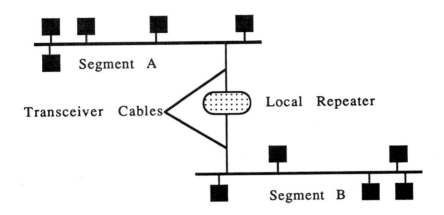

A Local Repeater Configuration

In many Ethernet hardware controllers (the board on the processor attached to the Ethernet), there exists a data recording mode called "promiscuous mode." When a controller is placed in promiscuous mode by a program, it will capture every packet it sees and send the packets up to a destination program for further processing. Promiscuous mode is passive (no emanations from the node in promiscuous mode are emitted), therefore no other node will know that the node in promiscuous mode will be listening in on the data being sent on the Ethernet. Further, since the Ethernet (any variety) is broadcast oriented, any message sent to any node on an Ethernet is immediately seen by all nodes. As a result, data capture of all packets on an Ethernet is fairly straightforward, especially if a controller has the ability to support promiscuous mode.

One obvious side effect of promiscuous mode is that if a node is in it, it can see all traffic. This can pose a security problem in some environments, especially if the station collecting the data is a PC with a programmer with some knowledge attached to it.

A reasonably talented programmer could easily capture packets on the network and break out the DATA section of the packet into something intelligible. Since most software packages do not encrypt the DATA section of the packet, it is quite simple for a programmer to break out the packet and capture usernames, passwords, and sensitive data. The bad part is that since promiscuous mode is passive, no other station knows about the transgression.

This feature is what makes a repeater useful. A repeater collects all traffic on each segment by, basically, utilizing controller features for each segment and collecting data in promiscuous mode. Data from one segment (which we shall call A) is collected in the repeater and sent out on the opposite segment (B). Conversely, data is collected on B and sent up, intact and without translation, to A. A repeater simply repeats data. No more, no less.

In the local configuration, the repeater is connected to the transceivers on each segment via transceiver cables. This is the limiting factor on how far apart the Ethernet segments can be from each other. Most vendors only allow transceiver cables to be no more than 50 meters in length. If this were used, then the segments could be no more than 100 meters from each other. In local configurations, this is usually more than adequate for connectivity purposes.

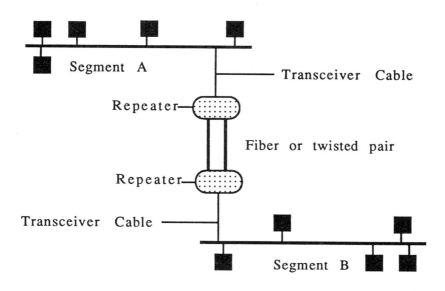

A Remote Repeater Configuration

A remotely connected repeater involves the use of, usually, two repeaters. Each repeater is connected to its Ethernet segment with a transceiver and a transceiver cable, but the two repeaters are connected to each other via twisted pair cable, fiber optic cables, or, possibly, MODEMs and phone links. When twisted pair are used, the maximum speed between repeaters is usually limited to T1 (1.544Mbps). When fiber is used, the speed is limited by the fiber optic MODEMs used. In addition to the speed of the connection, there is usually a distance limitation between repeater boxes as well (many have about 1000 meters of distance between repeater units). You will need to consult the repeater vendor for specific information regarding connection distance and supported connec--tion media.

Different Kinds of Repeaters

What has been previously described is a run-of-the-mill, garden variety repeater configuration. Local and remote connections with repeaters are available from a great many Ethernet component vendors and come in a variety of styles and prices. Some of the smarter repeaters can generate metrics and load information and many other useful accounting and statistical features

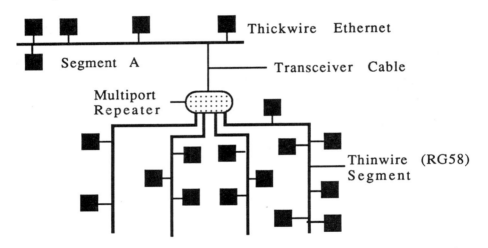

A Multiport Repeater with Four Thinwire Segments

One type of repeater that has not before been mentioned, however, is the type known as a multiport repeater. A multiport repeater is configured in a manner similar to a local repeater: it is tapped into the Ethernet segment via a transceiver and transceiver cable. Instead of connecting to another Ethernet segment, the multiport repeater allows multiple Ethernet segments, usually RG58 thinwire segments, to directly connect to the multiport repeater.

The most popular multiport repeaters act as hub connections to eight or more Ethernet segments. In the case of thinwire, each thinwire segment may be connected to the repeater box with each thinwire segment allowing connection of about 30 nodes. In this manner, a single multiport repeater would allow up to 240 nodes to be connected to the eight thinwire segments with the repeater itself connected to the thickwire segment. The multiport repeater does the exact same thing as the locally configured or remotely configured repeaters: repeat all traffic between all segments connected to the multiport repeater. A major difference is, however, most multiport repeaters may only be configured in a local manner and usually may not be directly connected to another repeater.

A final useful feature is that all connected segments are electrically isolated from each other. This means that while the segments connected to the multiport repeater give the illusion of being one BIG Ethernet, in reality, from an electrical point of view, the segments are still separate and isolated. This is useful should a segment fail: no other segment will be affected except for those which have nodes wishing to communicate with nodes on the failed segment.

Repeater Rules of Configuration

Configuring repeaters is fairly simple, but there are a few configuration rules that must be followed.

First, most vendors impose what is called the "two-repeater rule." This translates to the restriction that the path from any one node to any other node may not go through more than two repeaters. The reasons for this vary, but it is usually attributed to the problems of propagation delay of traffic between communicating remote nodes on different segments of coaxial Ethernet.

Another rule frequently seen is the homogeneity rule. Repeaters for a certain type of 802 network (such as 802.3 - Ethernet) may only connect to a like network. In other words, most repeaters for Ethernets may only connect Ethernets together; they may not also connect to, say, an 802.5 token ring. Some vendors have boxes that allow such feats of wonderment and daring. These types of boxes, however, are usually called translation bridges or gateways as they bridge or act as a gateway between the networks (there must be a translation of packet type in the box, not a simple repeat of traffic from one network to another). Most bridges do NOT translate between two types of network protocols. Only special translation bridges will.

A final rule has to do with cable distancing between repeaters and segments. These vary greatly from vendor to vendor, so consult your favorite vendor for details.

There may be more rules imposed depending upon the repeater system selected. In all cases, consult the vendor and get the information from same. You may have to dig a bit for information as well; not all personnel at all vendors know all the intricacies of Ethernet configuration.

Bridges are Not Repeaters. Sort of.

A bridge looks very similar to a repeater. In fact, they are configured practically identically (from some vendors, absolutely identically) as a repeater is configured in local and remote configuration cases. A bridge also allows the Ethernet segments being connected together to appear as one large Ethernet to all attached nodes. The main difference between a bridge and a repeater is how traffic is handled: a bridge is a selective repeater.

Selective repeating of traffic means that only traffic that is actually destined for a node on the opposite segment is repeated from one segment to another. This has several distinct advantages:

1. Only traffic that needs to go to the opposite segment actually is repeated to it. This reduces overall traffic load on the opposite segment.
2. Security is increased as not all segments hooked together with bridges will see all traffic from all segments.
3. Most bridge units are very "smart." That is, they can be programmed to react in certain ways and allow certain types of connectivity matrices. Also, certain node addresses may be screened out to keep unwanted traffic from being propagated to other segments.

Bridges do not necessarily have to conform to the same configuration rules that repeaters must. Depending upon vendor rules, a node may be able to connect to a remote node that may be as far away as seven bridge units. Also, there may be intermediate repeaters between the bridge units. Accordingly, the network configured with bridges and repeaters may have many segments connecting many nodes together where the entire configuration looks like one large Ethernet.

In many situations, Ethernet bridges use a traffic-routing technique known as a spanning tree. Not all bridges use this technique, but the technique is quite powerful and flexible. Through the use of spanning tree, bridges may "learn" about the segment topologies and the existence of other bridges. As a result, traffic will not be transmitted in a redundant fashion between segments, and two segments may be connected to each other through two or more bridges for redundancy purposes. In this manner, a bridge may be very useful. Repeaters cannot be used is such a manner, as data would be sent in a terminal loop between the segments. With the spanning-tree capability, bridges learn about one another and are capable of functioning in a redundant method.

Some vendors manufacture bridge units that are capable of being connected to remote bridge units through leased telephone lines, X.25 packet switch interfaces (PSDNs), fiber, or satellite communications channels. This allows Ethernets in different locations (in other cities, states, or countries) to be connected together as one big happy Ethernet.

All this capability is not without cost. Bridge units tend to be substantially more expensive that repeaters and units that resemble a multiport repeater are very specialized and expensive indeed - sometimes prohibitively so. Bridges, therefore, are usually used where the installation of a bridge (or bridges) can reduce the traffic load between segments significantly enough to justify the expense. In some network topologies (such as when the two repeater rule becomes a problem in layout), the bridge units will be required for the network to function properly and, in those cases, will be included automatically.

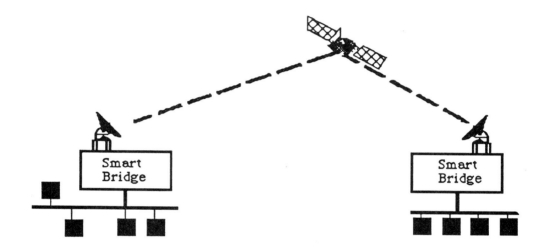

A Satellite Bridge Configuration

One problem with bridges is that they are inherently slower than repeaters. To provide spanning-tree capability and traffic filtering requires some serious overhead in the bridge system. As such, they are slower than repeaters and may cause traffic flow problems between segments. To help combat this problem, some manufacturers have allowed their bridge systems to connect to more than one communications link between Ethernet segments. While this seems like a reasonable approach, it can cause problems that are not of the bridges doing. For example, some Ethernet protocols are very simple in nature and do not allow for retransmission or packet sequencing. Therefore, if packets were purged (discarded) due to bridge congestion, the data stream to a particular machine would be disrupted, and the link may be aborted by the software on either side. Further, if packets arrived out of sequence due to the routing capability of the bridge units being used, the system software on the remote side may cause the link to be destroyed due to packet arrival being out of proper sequence. Use of a smart bridge is desirable in many situations, but if the network is improperly configured from a data flow point of view or if the bridge units purge or resequence traffic because of congestion, there can be severe repercussions on throughput and individual system performance. Capabilities of bridges must be carefully considered and combined with known traffic flow details to insure a fully functional interconnection situation.

In summary, bridges are very good for traffic reduction but need to be carefully considered. If the primary traffic path is node-to-node and the communicating nodes are all on the same segment, a bridge is a wise choice and will provide effective service. If, however, the traffic is node-to-node and the nodes are on different segments, the bridge is then functioning as no more than an expensive repeater. A bridge may still be warranted in this type of configuration if the network manager wishes to restrict certain nodes from connecting to remote systems on another segment.

To Serve, To Serve

Yet another type of system found on Ethernets is a server. A server is usually a dedicated system of some sort that provides connectivity services to printer resources, disk resources, file resources, or terminal resources. Some servers have their own local operating system that is either stored on disk, tape, or in ROM. Many servers have their executable kernels loaded into them through a load request mechanism.

Downline System Loading

Ethernet is ideally suited to provide what is generically called "loading service." This is because of the broadcast nature of Ethernet and the ability to use group (multicast) addressing.

Many servers allow connection of classic data processing equipment such as asynchronous terminals, serial and parallel printers, and disk drives. To access such equipment from many nodes that are on the network, some sort of network access routines must be included in each server node as well as a local database to keep track of what component is talking to which machine and which program on the network. This can get very difficult on complex networks, so servers must have a good degree of intelligence to be of any use on any network. Having the "smarts" located on the server allows the server to be configured independently of any network entity, but it also requires that the server be active before any serious configuration modifications can be made. Another problem is that of updates. As remote systems change and get upgrades, servers must be upgraded to keep up with the remote systems. If all code is on the server, it must be upgraded which can be tedious and difficult. If the server code is located entirely in ROM, an upgrade may require replacement of components in the server, and that is a problem as well. To solve these issues, some vendors have opted to allow remote loading of software from a host somewhere on the network. This is called downline system loading.

In the server there is usually a ROM that has just enough software in it to know how to issue a multicast message on an Ethernet to a certain address. This address, usually called a multicast load assist address, is broadcast out by the server at server power-up. The packet requesting a load is broadcast on the network to all stations. Stations that know about the multicast load assist message will check their local network database to see if the node (the server) is a known machine, and whether or not the station that is reading the multicast message can assist in the load. If the station determines that it can successfully help out (in other words, the server is a known loadable entity), the station will send a message to the server telling the server that it is the loader and that it will be giving the server the information requested. The server sends an acknowledgement and the host begins to send the kernel down to the server. How the actual data transfer is done depends largely on the server type and the protocol being used to support the load to the server. Different host software packages, such as DECnet and some TCP/IP or XNS packages prescribe standard loading protocols as part of the supported protocol suite, so the remote would have to know how to understand the loading protocol from a particular software package for the load to work successfully.

Typically the load host (as the loading node is known) will know about the server before the load request from the server is broadcast. This is due to previous definition of the server in a loading database kept on nodes that know how to execute downline system loads. If there is more than one load host on the network, it is possible that more than one system will attempt to provide the load to the server. In this case, most major loading protocols allow for the remote to acknowledge one host and eventually the other answering hosts will discontinue their load assistance response after not having heard, directly, from the remote for a prescribed period of time.

Primary Load (ROM code on remote)
|
Secondary Load (from host)
|
Tertiary Load (from host)
|
System Load (from host)
|
Remote System Boots Up

Remote Node Operating System Load Sequence

Most loading systems use what is called a staged load. Staged loading means that the kernel that will eventually be used to run the server is loaded in pieces. Typically, the server executes locally installed ROM code to create the multicast load assist message.

47

This is called the primary load sequence. A secondary loader is sent from the load host to the server to allow the server to properly handle any incoming software packets, as the primary load ROM code is usually not sophisticated enough to allow this feature. The secondary loader then receives the tertiary loader from the host load system to allow further packet loading and to get ready to handle the system load. Finally, the operating kernel for the server is sent from the host to the server. The server will then execute a local bootstrap of the loaded kernel and the kernel will begin to execute. At this point the server is loaded.

The actual specifics on what message is sent at what time in what protocol is up to the software package being used to provide the downline system load. How DEC's Maintenance Operations Protocol (MOP) handles the load is radically different than the way that TCP/IP or XNS might. In all cases, however, the general sequence is the same.

The reason for the various load stages is fairly easy. By loading as much of the server software as possible from the host system, any modifications to the loaders or to the kernel may be easily made as most systems keep the loader software and server kernel in standard files on the host. New files with modifications and patches are easily inserted in the proper directories and the next time the server is loaded, the changes go into effect without having to open up the server, change ROM, or other such inconvenient job. If a new version of the server kernel is released, it is a simple manner to copy the new kernel file on to the host and force a re-boot of the server. In short, new features and capabilities, not to mention bug fixes, can be easily added without having to lobotomize the server to implement same.

Which host systems are allowed to load remote servers is strictly up to the vendor software and the network manager. What files the host systems will load in to the remote servers depends upon the same entities. In all cases, an improperly configured server or load host will cause the server not be loaded correctly and in turn cause other problems that will need to be solved.

In all situations, it is almost irrelevant as to the type of server that is being loaded with the exception of what files get sent and which protocol is being used. In all cases, practically any type of server can be downline system loaded providing the server and the remote host support the service.

Disk and File Servers

Most Ethernets that will be proliferated with Personal Computers (PCs, PSs, and Macintoshes) will usually end up with some sort of shared disk or file server. There is a difference between the two.

A disk server is a system that provides transparent connectivity to remote systems to a disk resource. In short, it is a disk that is "seen" by other systems on the network. A shared disk is a very useful thing in a network environment, as users can store financial models for spreadsheets, programs, data, mail messages, and a multitude of other items that help users get work accomplished. By using a sharable disk drive, users can share templates, data, etc., without having to do the "floppy shuffle" between systems. A network accessible disk server will typically allow the disk drive to look as if it were locally attached to a particular system when, in reality, it is on a disk server somewhere on the network. Since all connected systems view the disk as being local, it is an easy way to exchange data between systems as the data does not really move between systems, but various systems can see and access the common data on the disk.

Disk servers have some problems, though. The foremost one is what happens when two programs from two different nodes on the network try to access a particular file at the same time. To compound the problem, let's suppose that not only were the two programs trying to get to the file but also were trying to write to a particular record in that file at the same time. This could cause major problems as the server would have to coordinate which program on which remote system is trying to access which piece of data in which mode (read or write). This can get very difficult to manage and the software effort involved in providing such a feat is incredible! As such, a disk server usually allows various systems to access files on the disk, but after that what else is allowed depends upon the complexity of the software in the server and on the remote systems. Typically this means that remote system programs may access files in a "read" mode but only one program at a time on a particular remote system may "write" to the file. Some disk servers are even more primitive in that only one program from a particular node can have a particular file open for access at a time. If any other program on any other node wants to access the file, it must wait until the program currently accessing the desired file is finished.

File servers are very similar to disk servers in construction, but the features allowed are somewhat more advanced. File servers usually allow what is called record-level locking. This feature allows multiple programs from multiple remote nodes to access the same file at the same time in either a read mode, write mode, or both. When writing to the file, the file server insures that no two programs from any two remote systems can write to the exact same record in a file at the same time. By "locking" a record from multiple write access, potential corruptions of the file are eliminated and true sharing of disk and file resources is possible.

Which type of server is best for your needs is something that you will need to sit down and consider. The largest consideration is which operating systems support access to the disk server or file server and is there software available for each operating system that wishes to connect to the server for access. Some distributed file systems, such as Sun Computer's Network File System (NFS), are being supported both on servers and remote hosts, thus allowing any program on any machine to get at any file on any server or remote system that supports the NFS protocols and access methods. One of the more attractive things about NFS is the support garnered by larger computer vendors who plan on using NFS in their proprietary file systems to allow remote system access to the file system.

In short, disk and file servers are similar in architecture, but internal capabilities vary radically depending upon protocols, vendors, and application support. Selection of a disk or file server depends heavily upon application and the requirement for sharability of files.

Printer Servers

Printer servers are fairly easy to understand: a printer of some supported type is connected to a microprocessor-based server that knows how to connect to remote host systems. The variety of implementations of this technology are, however, staggering.

Some print servers consist of nothing more than a printer, an Ethernet interface, and some sort of ROM code that knows how to ask a host system for a print job and also how to report back status information. More sophisticated versions of the printer server actually have local disk support and can attach to many nodes and look local to those nodes. To accomplish this, host systems wishing to use the printer server will usually require some chunk of code on each host that knows how to access the printer as well as how to queue a request for a job to be printed on the distributed printer. While this seems fairly straightforward, it can get very nasty when you are considering the myriad of laser printer fonts, forms, styles, and paper types that can be specified in each print job. Multiply that by the number of nodes that know how to access the printer server and you can see how something simple turns complex very quickly.

Printer servers are very useful when an expensive printer resource, such as a laser printer, is available, and multiple systems would like to connect and use the resource. If the printer is a cheap printer (such as the very inexpensive dot matrix or ink-jet printers), putting in the server software and hardware would cost infinitely more than placing a printer on each connected system. A real question floating around is the issue of dropping costs on laser printers. If a laser printer becomes inexpensive enough to put one on each machine, why invest the time, money, and aggravation of installing printer servers? Good point.

Printer servers, with the exception of large and expensive printers, typically are an included or, at a minimum, optional feature on most disk and file servers. A few companies make dedicated printer servers for Ethernet, but most printer servers are part of a disk or file server package. Some companies are offering dedicated network printers with Ethernet interfaces, but these printers are usually proprietary to a particular vendor and its technologies and are not globally used by all systems on the network.

Terminal Servers

During the testing of the 3Mbps Ethernet in the late 70's, a number of performance test results suggested, strongly, that terminal traffic not be used on an Ethernet due to its short duration, overhead, and extremely bursty nature of flow. This was due, however, to protocols that were not optimized for the Ethernet environment. While it is still true that terminal traffic is not the best thing to place on an Ethernet, newer protocols developed specifically for terminal traffic and improved host handling of terminal traffic have made terminal server technology very appealing to a great many businesses.

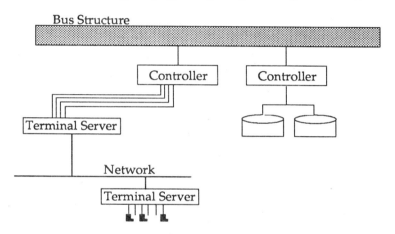

Terminal Servers as Stand-alone Multiplexers

The first types of terminal servers functioned as glorified multiplexer boxes. Terminals were attached to a source server, and a destination server was connected, directly, to a particular host system. All servers were instructed, via software commands, what servers they were allowed to connect to and which ports on which servers were computer ports. This configuration effort was tedious and time consuming. In effect, the earlier concepts of a terminal server was that of a port selector unit or what is now frequently referred to as a data PBX. Terminals connected to one side, systems connected to the other, and virtual connections were made between the two. The terminals thought they were connected to a system and the systems thought there were terminals directly connected to the systems. In short, early terminal servers provided connection between terminals and systems by functioning as a multiplexer and using Ethernet as the media between the multiplexers.

With further understanding of the Ethernet environment came developments in the handling of terminal I/O on Ethernet. Some vendors, such as Digital Equipment Corporation, developed specific terminal protocol types for terminal servers. This development proved useful, as the overall technique of multiplexing did not change in concept, but

51

changed in execution. In the DEC implementation, a protocol called Local Area Transport (LAT) was produced by the terminal server and sent to a destination host system. Instead of using another terminal server on the host side connected to existing terminal hardware ports, the LAT packet from Ethernet was sent to a special de-multiplexing software (called the LT device driver) component in the destination system's operating system. At that point the terminal packet was passed to a virtual terminal port and the session complete. The destination system "thinks" there is a terminal directly attached, but, in reality, the virtual terminal is a software component. Through this method of

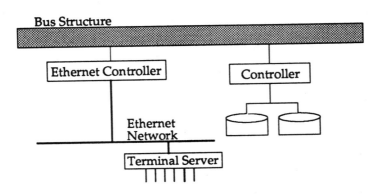

terminal serving, less actual hardware is used, and more sessions can be supported.

Terminal Server Implementation With a Remote LAT Multiplexer

With many terminal servers, printers are supported as valid print devices. When the two-server concept is used, a printer is set up as a serial printer on a dedicated terminal port on a particular system. This usually means that a particular system can access the printer, but other systems may not be able to share the printer.

In the case of LAT, a printer may also be connected to a terminal server port, but since the host systems that can be connected to the terminal servers create virtual ports, the terminal server with a printer attached can "poll" remote host systems for print jobs. This allows a printer on a particular terminal port on a particular server to be shared amongst many different systems that know how to use the LAT protocol when accessing a printer on a remote server.

Chapter Summary

Repeaters and bridges are very useful devices to connect segments of Ethernet together in a useful, cohesive fashion. By selection and installation of specific kinds of repeaters and bridges in complementary configurations, an Ethernet's total length can far exceed the standard prescribed 2.5Km total length restriction.

Servers help utilize the Ethernet resource in a shared way. Used with bridges and repeaters, many distant systems can connect to the resources in a straightforward fashion. Selection of bridges when using servers can assist in restricting traffic load between segments and allow better performance of the Ethernet as a whole.

Different vendors implement servers in different ways. In all cases, servers can be a great help in sharing and distributing information as well as sharing expensive resources such as laser printers and disks. Through the judicious use of servers, a business may realize a more useful Ethernet in terms of functionality and configuration.

Chapter Five

Personal Computers
and Ethernet

It is nonsense to say there is not enough time to be fully informed...Time given to thought is the greatest timesaver of all.

Norman Cousins

Introduction

In the race to get "networked" many companies are taking the personal computer (PC) resource in-house and connecting them in various ways to effectively utilize existing resources. Another major reason is to spread the knowledge base around in a company. Knowledge base is the overall pool of knowledge a company has in its employees. Some analysts estimate that less than 10% of the available knowledge in a company is used properly. By using networks to connect workstations and employees together, the knowledge base utilization in a company may be more effectively utilized.

In this chapter we shall explore the various ways in which PCs may be connected to Ethernet. Remember, however, that personal computers no longer are restricted to the IBM PC, clones, or look-alikes. The Apple Macintosh is starting to make a sizable dent in some companies and other products in the future will have a similar effect. So, this chapter refers to PCs and Ethernet, but not necessarily IBM PCs only.

What is Required for Most PC Networks?

In most situations, a PC network happens from the desire to connect various PCs together to share a disk, share a printer, or, possibly, exchange mail and other types of information. Unfortunately, network products do not always live up to expectations. A PC network may end up being comprised of a collection of differing hardware and software products that allow the users to perform the tasks that they needs.

To provide the facilities desired, the basic components involved consist of a wire plant, interface hardware, and software. In some cases, additional specialized hardware such as dedicated disk and print servers or gateways to other networks or bridges to similar, but remote, networks. While it seems that the parts list is small, that is not the half of the problem. Getting all the parts to cooperate is the major issue at hand.

Obviously, the hardware selection is not trivial. How do you pick out THE product from the morass of offerings in the marketplace? Ask any vendor and they will tell you what you need: their product. Since we are looking at using Ethernet for our solution, the problem is simplified somewhat: instead of having to pick from 500 products, you now only have to select THE product from 300 products. What a relief!

Even with Ethernet, there are problems in selection. Let's discuss the differing types of Ethernet and where each fits in.

Thin Wire Ethernets

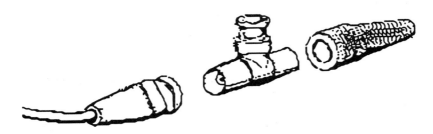

An RG58 "T" Connection

One the first cable plants to consider is the thin wire plant. Why? It is flexible, easy to install, and can support a fair number of nodes (most thinwire vendors allow 30 nodes or less on a 189-meter thinwire segment). Since most office environments are less than 189 meters in total length and usually have less than 20 nodes, the thinwire solution seems like a reasonable approach. It has its drawbacks, however.

Thinwire cable (RG58 R/U coax, 50 ohm, terminated) must be intrusively tapped. This means that if a connection is to be made to the cable, the cable must physically be cut in half and a "T" connector inserted in-line with the cable. While this is not difficult to do, it does cause a disruption of the cable and the network will be down until the tap is complete. Typically a female BNC connector is installed on each end of the severed cable. The two ends are connected together by inserting a metal T connector that has two male ends (for the two female connectors installed on each end of the Ethernet) and one female end for connecting on to the PC. Taps are usually eight or more feet apart.

After the thinwire is tapped, the PC controller (located in the PC) is connected to the cable. On the back of most PC cards that communicate with Ethernet is a male BNC connector that is used to connect to the T that was installed on the Ethernet thinwire. Because of electrical considerations, the controller must be directly connected to the wire, and a cable drop from the T to the controller is typically not allowed. Connection is simple - simply push the female end of the T onto the male connector on the PC and twist to the right. The connector will seat, and the PC is now on the network.

It is important to point out that some vendors of Ethernet for PCs allow configurations different than the standard described earlier. 3COM Corporation, with its various 3Plus and Etherseries products, allows slightly differing configurations depending upon what software is being run and what type of hardware configuration has been selected. Certain 3COM Ethernets allow thinwire configurations of 1000 feet per segment with 100 node taps on the segment. Additionally, nodes may be tapped as close together as three (3) feet which is much closer than the recommended eight feet. This variance in configuration demonstrates both the flexibility and frustration of PC networks with Ethernet. With all the products available to allow Ethernet connectivity, there are practically as many different configuration rules.

One of the biggest problems with thinwire connections is people. Yes, people. People pulling connectors loose by pulling on PCs. People tripping over thinwire cable and tearing up terminators and connectors. People taking their PC home for the weekend and disconnecting the PC from the network by twisting loose the two female connectors on the ends of the Ethernet cable rather than properly disconnecting the single female end of the connector from the back of the male BNC connector protruding from the PC. It is very important to remember that the thinwire Ethernet is close to users and, as such, can be easily disrupted. Connectors should be placed in plastic housings so that users cannot mess with the connectors without getting in contact with knowledgeable systems personnel. Warning stickers are very useful as well. In short, thinwire is susceptible to easy disruption and care must be taken to insure that it doesn't happen because of carelessness or ignorance.

How fast is thinwire? 10Mbit/sec, just like the thickwire. Why is it popular? Ease of installation and ease of upgrade.

Thinwire Ethernets may also be connected to thickwire Ethernets either directly (through a barrel connector) or through a repeater or bridge. If the connection is made directly, care should be taken to understand the following points:

1. Thinwire is subject to disruption by users. If the thinwire becomes part of the overall Ethernet and is not connected via a "box," then if the thinwire receives a disruption, so does the thickwire. Any break in the cable on either side will cause total network failure. While the thick to thin connection works and works well, it can cause serious ulcers when the network dies because some user disconnected his PC incorrectly and decides to take it home. While this may not seem to be critical, it is. Locating a break in an Ethernet is a hassle. If the break is in a sea of cubicles, the problem really compounds substantially.

2. The overall supportable wire distance changes. If a network is 75% thick and 25% thin, that profile presents different electrical characteristics than the situation of being 25% thick and 75% thin. Why? Simple. Electrical characteristics and noise issues change as the length and capabilities or the cable change. As a result, a network of mostly thick wire has different tolerances and electrical characteristics than does a network of mostly thin wire. In other words, the overall length allowed becomes shorter as the relative amount of thinwire vs. thickwire increases. If the network is mostly thickwire, the network may be allowed to be longer, but it is up to the vendor. For an example on how to compute thinwire distances, consult Chapter Three.

3. If a bridge or a repeater is to be used, insure that you understand the capabilities and restrictions of the product involved. Some repeaters allow up to eight thinwire segments to be connected to a single thickwire. Some repeaters only allow one thickwire to be connected to one thinwire. Other devices segment the two networks by utilizing the repeater or bridge as a terminator of sorts. This means that if either side of a segment goes down, the other side of the segment does not fail and nodes on the working side may still communicate with each other. Some networks are designed with this particular capability in mind.

I typically recommend that in situations where a thin wire is to be connected to a thick wire, use a repeater or a bridge. The additional expense for such a device is usually made up for in the lower total network downtime and lower consumption of ulcer medicine. On multi-port repeaters (repeaters capable of supporting multiple segments), the additional expense also allows a fairly good expansion capability without a major reconfiguration of the network.

Thinwire is pretty easy to run and tap (intrusively) into. Remember that there is a segment distance limitation of at least 189 meters per segment and about 30 nodes, depending upon the vendor of the thinwire controllers for the PC's.

Thickwire and PCs

PC's hook up fine to thickwire as well. As with other types of nodes on thickwire, the cable must be tapped and a transceiver attached. This causes a bit of concern as many PC Ethernet controllers have two connectors built into the controller. The first connector is the thinwire BNC male connected previously discussed. The second connector is a 15- pin transceiver cable connector. The reason for the second connector is due to the fact that many Ethernet PC controllers not only have two connectors, they also have a built-in transceiver. Normally the units are shipped with the transceiver enabled so that the controller can be directly attached to a thinwire (just because the controller is attached directly to the thinwire does not obviate the need for a transceiver). If the controller is to be attached to a thickwire or to an Ethernet medium that requires the transceiver to be directly attached to the medium, the controller's DIP switches must be set to disable the on-board transceiver mechanism and utilize an off-board transceiver. In the case of thickwire Ethernet, transceivers must be directly attached so an off-board transceiver must be used which is connected to the 15-pin D connector on the back of the controller.

It is important to remember that thickwire Ethernet has distance limitations on segment length as well. Cable taps cannot be any closer than 2.5 meters and there is a limitation of 100 taps per 500 meter segment. This means that trying to get a large population of PCs on a thickwire can be very difficult. Another issue is the cable itself. Thickwire is not very flexible and can be difficult to lay out in an office environment. As a rule, a thickwire cable works fine, but is not recommended for large concentrations of PCs.

Twisted Pair Ethernet

Some companies have introduced 10Mbit Ethernet capabilities on 24-gauge unshielded twisted pair telephone cable. Ethernet works the same on the twisted pair as it does on thinwire and thickwire; the connectors, however, are necessarily different. Some vendors provide connectors that are similar in nature to standard telephone RJ11 or RJ45 jacks. Some vendor's implementations hook stations together from station to station in a total segment distance usually not to exceed 70-100 meters depending upon the vendor of the twisted pair plant. In such implementations, the hookup points may support more than one PC connection (some connect up to six). The segments of twisted pair may then be connected to a hub device (possibly as many as 48 twisted pair segments), such as a twisted pair multiport repeater, which may, in turn, connect the twisted pair segments up to a thickwire or fiber optic backbone segment in a manner similar to a thinwire multiport repeater. Other vendor implementations connect a single twisted pair to each station and then connect each station to a hub repeater in a "star" network fashion. The hubs may then be connected together either through thinwire, thickwire, fiber, or twisted pair connections, forming the network.

This type of Ethernet medium is not for all environments, but it is especially suitable for companies that are implementing AT&T's twisted pair and fiber Premises Distribution System (PDS). Care in implementation must be exercised, however. Twisted pair systems that communicate at high speed are limited in length and configuration due to DC loop resistance problems and the AC attenuation of the twisted pairs. Twisted pair also are more susceptible to radiation of radio frequency (RF) interference. Careful adjustment of cable lengths and cable placement is very important for the proper functionality of the network and to keep the unwanted RF interference and electrical distortions to a minimum.

At the time of this writing, IEEE 802.3 subcommittee 10BaseT, the committee responsible for the impending twisted pair standard, has begun working on a twisted pair 802.3 baseband standard. Agreements between participants include a network capable of 100 meters length, 10Mbps speed, and an attached unit interface (AUI). There has been considerable discussion between the vendors as to whether systems may be daisy chained or not, but no definitive answers have been reached. In short, there is no standard on twisted pair Ethernet at this writing and there will most likely be considerable differences between current vendor implementations and the actual produced standard.

PC Broadband Ethernet

Some vendors use a thinwire coaxial approach for a PC network, but utilize a broadband technology rather than the less expensive baseband. This has advantages: broadband is typically less susceptible to interference than baseband (which is useful in factory or industrial environments), can allow many connections, and provides connectivity facilities over and above the Ethernet data connection services. In fact, one vendor has promoted, heavily, a PC network based upon broadband technology but configured only for situations where mostly PC's will be used: IBM.

The PC Network from IBM is actually a broadband Ethernet technology developed by Sytek. The system allows 72 nodes to be connected to a broadband coax network that is not over a 1000 foot radius. Nodes are usually connected to network hub units called eight-way splitters that allow up to eight PCs to be connected at distances from 25 feet to 200 feet away from the splitter. Splitters are then connected together through directional broadband taps to a base expansion unit that can control eight splitters. The base expansion unit is an add-on unit that is attached to a device called a translation unit. The function of the translation unit is to take the transmitted data on the "send" channel (50.75 MHz) and repeat the information to the "receive" channel (219.00 MHz). Since the PC Network is a broadband technology, all frequencies used for data transmission are typically unidirectional - nodes cannot send and receive on the same channel on the cable. As such, the two channels are used to transmit information. A sending node transmits its data on 50.75 MHz and then listens to 219.00 MHz to insure that it went out OK. If not (the packet it sees that it sent is garbled or does not match what was sent), it presumes a collision, backs off, and retries again later, just like baseband networks. The translation unit, in addition to "translating" the send frequency to the receive frequency, also has room for eight local connections to PCs (again, the PCs can be 25-200 feet away from the connection point), allowing a total number of connections to the network of 72 (eight splitters plus the eight nodes on the translator unit).

In addition to the cabling method used for the PC Network, the controllers used are special in that they contain a device function known as an RF MODEM. Radio Frequency (RF) MODEMs are used to take digital data and modulate (send) the digital signals in an analog form on a cable media or other such transmission method. The remote side demodulates the signal and converts it back to digital data that the system can understand. While this sounds all well and good, there is the problem of broadband networks of signal strengths and potential distortion problems. Signal strength is an issue as broadband networks are easily affected by cable distances between signal amplifiers or other nodes. It's like listening to a radio. If you are very close to the radio, you may feel that it is too loud and cannot hear what is being broadcast very well as the signal is distorted. If, however, you back away a certain distance, the radio now becomes intelligible. Back still further away and the signal emitted by the radio may be too weak to hear, which is just as bad as being to close and the signal is "overdriven." RF-based networks (broadband) work much the same way. If a station is too close to the amplification source (in this case the eight-way splitters or translation unit), the signal from the adjacent system could be too loud. If the system is too far away, the signal may be too weak. As such, the PC Network has some fairly rigid cable distance restrictions to keep from having to play games with the network to get it to function properly when configured.

Broadband PC networks are very useful and powerful, but there are some planning issues to be decided and installation and/or configuration restrictions that MUST be observed if the network is to function correctly.

PC Ethernet Controllers

Ethernet controllers are available for practically any type of computer these days. A great many vendors manufacture controllers, but not all controllers support all cable types or software protocols.

By and large, Ethernet controllers for the IBM PC, PS/2 and compatibles will plug straight into the system bus in a manner similar to any other type of controller (such as that for a disk, printer, video adapter, etc.). Most controllers also come with a software package that, at a minimum, provides an installation guide and software device driver that allows system software to "talk" to the controller. Some vendors are starting to produce Ethernet controllers that may also plug into the Small Computer Systems Interface (SCSI) bus that many personal computer manufacturers support.

On the Macintosh computer line, vendors provide Ethernet controllers that plug straight into the NuBus peripheral bus on the Mac II and the SE. For the Mac Plus, Ethernet controllers are available for the SCSI port. Still other vendors provide an off-system box that provides Ethernet connectivity on one side and interfaces to the Mac serial port in the other side. As with the IBM PC, PS/2, and clones, driver and support software is usually included, as is an installation guide.

In all cases, installation of the PC, PS and Mac hardware is not difficult for the mechanically minded, but may void your system's warranty. Check with your respective vendor before installation to make sure that whoever installs the system hardware does so in accordance with specifications prescribed by the Ethernet controller vendor and system manufacturer. Carefully read the instructions on hardware installation, set any switch options on the controller before installation, and follow the instructions carefully. Always make sure that the system is turned off and disconnected from any power source and take care not to touch any of the chips on the card unless you are well grounded. Touching the card directly may cause a static discharge that can damage components on the card. Handle the card by its edges and carefully insert the card into its respective bus firmly but NEVER force it into the bus slot. Most cards align and insert easily, so difficulty in alignment or insertion may indicate other problems. Once the card is inserted into the system, attach either the Ethernet or transceiver cable to the controller and replace any covers on the equipment.

Once the controller is installed, it is a good idea to secure any external cables either to the system with plastic tie wraps or in some manner that will preclude them being accidentally pulled away from the system. While it is quite true that the 15-pin D connector may be held on via a slide latch or screws or the thinwire connected via BNC connector, it is still highly recommended to secure the cable and connectors well to the system as users will move the system around and that can cause inadvertent cable disconnections and possible network faults. Better safe than sorry.

If the cable plant utilizes a fairly high-powered broadband system, it might also be wise to have RF leakage checked around the connection points between the PC and the network. RF, while not necessarily hazardous to humans (if a light enough amount), can cause other electrical components very serious and bizarre problems. Many vendors have RF leakage testers and they are readily available for rental from most instrumentation equipment rental shops.

The Software Connection/Contention

The final step in the installation of a PC on an Ethernet is the selection and installation of the networking software on the system. Some vendors will provide networking software with their Ethernet card, other vendors simply provide the hardware and a device driver to communicate to the card; the user of the system must find a suitable communications package that will solve his/her problem in an adequate manner.

Selection of a package depends a great deal upon the needs of a company. A small company with only PCs may require nothing more than a common package that runs on all systems and provides sharable disk resources. As the network needs grow, additional packages may be added to provide electronic mail, file transfer, shared printers, and many other capabilities. In the case where dissimilar types of PCs (IBM and Apple or others) are being networked together, the problems of file system compatibility, command compatibility, and other issues must be considered. Some companies are making a nice living providing such capabilities, but companies that specialize in PC-to-PC communications on Ethernet between like and dissimilar PCs are growing quickly.

In addition to the problems of PC-to-PC is the problem of PC-to-large system. Some of the early Ethernet host systems, such as VAX systems running VMS or UNIX and other UNIX-based systems that support Ethernet (such as AT&T 3B systems) have been able to communicate with each other for some time. Compatibility with PC systems, however, has been limited and is finally starting to grow and gain momentum. Solutions vary from custom PC to large system communications solutions to implementations of popular solutions, such as DECnet and TCP/IP on PCs to allow connectivity between the PCs and already supported larger minicomputers, superminicomputers, and mainframes. While this may seem like a reasonable recourse for some sites that are heavily committed to a particular software technology, such packages don't come cheap and sometimes may not solve the issues a company buys an Ethernet to solve. Examine the features of each package carefully and select one that is proven, extensible, and provides the features that are desired.

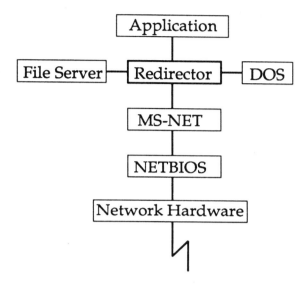

IBM PC NETBIOS Architecture

In most cases, software packages on IBM PCs will utilize an 8K series of network access routines available in ROM called NETBIOS (NETwork Basic Input-Output System). The purpose of NETBIOS (interrupt 2Ah or 5Ch, although 2Ah is recommended for future compatibility) is to provide programming and architecture personnel a standardized method and interface to all IBM network features and resources. Typically, NETBIOS is implemented on the network adapter (controller) card that gets plugged into a PC and provides connectivity to network resources.

The easiest way to describe NETBIOS is to look at it like an electronic traffic officer. As programs execute on the local machine, there are occasions when users may desire to access remote printers, disks, or other resources. NETBIOS detects the request for remote access and works with the network to connect the user to the remote resource. The remote NETBIOS on the remote PC takes the request and transfers it to the BIOS on the remote system for service. Upon service, the remote BIOS passes the information back to the remote NETBIOS which, in turn, passes the requested information back to the originating NETBIOS and eventually back to the user. While it seems somewhat tedious to access remote resources in this way, it actually is fairly efficient. Where it gets inefficient is when a particular system is very popular; then, delays are felt.

Accessing the interrupt routines provided by NETBIOS is not difficult, nor is it trivial. To facilitate the access to the network primitives in NETBIOS, Microsoft Corporation created a product called MS-NET, a higher-level interface to NETBIOS than using direct interrupt calls to the NETBIOS routines. MS-NET is typically not sold to end users. It is viewed as a developer's tool that allows access to the features and capabilities of NETBIOS regardless of the network architecture being implemented. IBM uses a highly modified version of MS-NET in its implementation of the IBM PC Network as well as the PC implementation of the 802.5 compatible token ring. Typically, a computer vendor implementing a particular network architecture on a PC that wished it to be supported, generically, between different types of network hardware, such as Ethernet and the 802.5 token ring, would code the application to know how to access MS-NET and let MS-NET worry about how to communicate to the controller (which, in turn, is connected to the network). Some vendors not wishing to pay licenses to Microsoft for the MS-NET code interface have developed their own compatible interface. As with any compatible interface, it is important to understand that not all situations may have been planned for by the compatible implementor, so caveat emptor: let the buyer beware!

Selection of software also brings with it the inevitable memory demands that will be imposed by the software. In the PC world, 640K is the maximum memory allowed in a supported DOS configuration. In O/S 2, the memory support facilities are greatly improved, but so is the memory utilization. In short, if you think your PC is tight for memory, just wait until the network software is installed! Some network packages require very little memory to execute properly; others cannot even start with less than 384Kb! Utilization of network facilities with an application running on a PC brings home the age old problem of how to fit five pounds of dirt into a 1 pound bag. It's tough to do and requires a LOT of mirrors.

A PC network usually consists of various PCs of various configurations. As such, there can be problems with which PC can support which function based upon PC compute power, network overhead, software overhead to access the resource, and many other variables. Normally, access of local resources can be draining to some PC types, depending upon hardware factors (disk speed, processor clock rate, MIPS rating of the processor chip, etc.), software factors (program language choice, operating system overhead, which system subroutine calls are being used, etc.), and task at hand (computation-intensive, I/O intensive, etc.). Selection of which PC is to perform what task on the network is very important if the network is to operate smoothly and efficiently.

For instance, if a PC/XT were chosen to serve as a disk server node due to a large amount of available disk, this might, at first, seem like a reasonable thing to do. If, however, the requests for disk access were coming from remote ATs or more powerful PS/2s, it is quite possible that the XT could become quickly swamped and unable to provide good response locally much less remotely. As a result all nodes accessing the

XT would be degraded as they would have to wait for the XT to sort out the requests and provide the needed information.

In a switch situation, let's say that a PS/2 Mod 80 were selected to serve as the disk server. While it is quite true that the PS/2 Mod 80 is much more powerful than the XT and could handle the additional load more easily, some consideration needs to be paid to the problem of what the PS/2 is doing. If a heavy-duty financial model is being run at the same time other nodes are trying to access disk and other resources on the PS/2, there could be a contention problem just as serious as the one previously described with the XT. The problem boils down to this: what is being run at what node, how often, and which system is trying to get to what resource has a dramatic effect on how the network will function and the overall throughput of the network.

In general terms, tests on various types of PC Ethernet configurations have shown that an AT server system (one providing services to other attached nodes) tends to be at least 30 percent faster depending upon traffic load. Also, the selection of software has a dramatic effect as well. In any case, proper placement of software components is critical to network throughput success.

One thing to consider when looking at PC/PS performance on Ethernet is modification of DOS parameters in the CONFIG.SYS file to allow for the heavier load that comes with a network. CONFIG.SYS is the DOS configuration file that is read at system boot time and that tells the system how much memory to allocate for functions, I/O sizes, known devices, and many other things. On a network, some of the standard system "parameters" may need to be modified to help the system along and allow for optimal performance. Which parameters will have to be modified are up to the vendor of the network, but modification of parameters can have a dramatic effect on network performance. Parameters such as disk buffers (BUFFERS=# of disk buffers to preallocate), file control blocks (FCBS=x,y) to allow more files to be open simultaneously, additional stacks (STACKS=x,y), etc., may need to be increased to allow the network to function properly with the PC and to get optimal performance.

When considering software access methods for the PC to get to Ethernet, there are other considerations besides the software technology chosen. Some nodes that need to communicate with certain types of systems, such as DEC VAX nodes, may be well advised to use packages such as DECnet. Others that wish to communicate frequently with UNIX nodes may need to run a TCP/IP-based package. In all situations, what software is run and which nodes are fulfilling what function will have a dramatic impact on how the Ethernet will respond to load.

In the area of software selection, software placement, utilization cycles, resource usage, and overhead, Macintosh systems incur much of the same concerns as the PC/PS systems do. With Macintosh, however, there are the additional problems of connectivity to the "closed" series of Macs (Mac Plus, 512KE, 512E, 512, and the venerable 128 - they have no general interface bus for peripherals), interface to the QuickDraw and other ROM routines, compatibility services if communicating with non-MAC systems on the same servers, and the Mac user interface which is radically different than the standard DOS interface (even when running Microsoft Windows). Things are looking up, however, for Macintoshes connected to Ethernet.

Application Layer	Application-specific protocols
Presentation Layer	AFP (filing protocol), Postscript
Session Layer	ASP (session protocol) and ADSP (stream protocol)
Transport Layer	ATP (transport protocol), Echo, NBP, ZIP
Network Layer	DDP (Datagram Delivery)
Data Link Layer	ALAP (Link Access Protocol)
Physical Layer	Twisted pair, coax, etc...

Appletalk Architecture

One company, Kinetics, (now owned by Excelan) has taken the market by storm by building a "bridge" product that allows the Apple Computer Appletalk network to connect to an Ethernet. Called FastPath, the Kinetics box allows Appletalk-based Macs and other Appletalk nodes to converse with Ethernet-based nodes, provided there is a level of software commonality between the two. Kinetics also makes other Ethernet interface products, such as a SCSI Ethernet interface, that allow Macintosh systems to connect to Ethernet straight up.

Bridging Appletalk to Ethernet is fine, but Appletalk is more than a twisted pair network. Appletalk has a layered protocol architecture that implements some fairly interesting protocols to provide shared disk services and other network primitives. Companies, such as Alisa Systems, have implemented the Appletalk protocols on non-Apple systems (such as the DEC VAX) system to allow the non-Apple systems and the Apple systems to share components (such as laser printers), disks, transfer files, etc. The problem with such connections, however, is not the software or Ethernet. The problem is with Appletalk. Appletalk is a 230Kbps network. Ethernet typically runs at

10Mbps. As a result, the network access is slow between Ethernet and Appletalk, not necessarily because of software or processor restrictions as much as because of speed issues with the Appletalk product. Placing Mac systems directly on Ethernet helps the throughput measurably, but then comes the problem of the network being faster than the ability of the Mac to process the data being sent to it or requested from it. At that point, the Mac exhibits the same issues discussed earlier in regard to PCs: what resource is placed on what node and which systems are accessing it, etc...

One of the problems with the Macintosh and Ethernet has been the lack of support of major network packages for the Macintosh. This is largely due to the "closed" nature of the system for so long (largely supplanted by the introduction of the Mac II with the IEEE-standardized NuBus I/O bus) as well as the difficulties involved in writing program code that works well with the Macintosh O/S interface (mouse-driven, pull-down menus). For the ease of use that the Macintosh provides, writing of code to provide the Macintosh "feel" is tedious and, often, difficult to do. Even experienced programmers resort to serious "hair pulling" when trying to use certain Mac features, so there is little wonder as to the delays involved.

This, however, is changing. The Macintosh, while not initially accepted as a "do-all" machine that IBM PC junkies claim the PC to be, has emerged as a powerful, well-rounded machine with an extensible architecture that fits well with Ethernet and other communications technologies. Accordingly, the Mac has emerged through the corporate underground as a workstation force to be reckoned with, especially in the desktop publishing environment for which the Mac practically created the market. This has created a corporate demand for products for Macintosh that allow the system to connect and share information with IBM PCs/PSs as well as corporate superminis and mainframes.

Companies such as Thursby Software Systems (TSS) have created products that allow the Mac to communicate not only on Ethernet but also through other network technologies. TSSNet, a product developed by TSS and marketed by Alisa Systems, provides a Digital Equipment Corporation DECnet-compatible communications architecture that features file transfer, virtual terminal support, and electronic mail facilities. Other companies are following suit and offering interconnection packages to existing Ethernet-based communications architectures. Packages supporting TCP/IP, XNS, and others are emerging rapidly and are making the Macintosh a viable workstation due to its interconnectivity capabilities in addition to its already superior graphics and user interface(s). Not to be left out, major vendors such as Apple, 3COM, Digital, AT&T, and others are getting into the act and providing Ethernet connectivity packages that allow the Mac to connect to a wide variety of diverse network configurations (including transparent access to PC/PS resources, not to mention mainframe and departmental resources) and Ethernet environments.

Chapter Summary

PC/PS/Macintosh connections to Ethernet are plentiful, easily done, and come in a variety of "flavors". In addition to the described methods, fiber connectivity is in the making and will soon, if not already, be available to hook up PCs to Ethernets. With such a selection of media and software solutions, there is a solution to most company desires in the Ethernet environment.

Chapter Six

Network Architecture and Software

Since we cannot know all that is to be known of everything, we ought to know a little about everything.

Blaise Pascal

Introduction

When the topic of networking comes up, some of the first things that get mentioned are network architecture and software. They're great buzzwords; they sound very official, impress management, and are good things to say when mentioning networks. Besides, when networking, do as the networkers do.

What is Network Architecture?

Network architecture is a fancy term for the way that networking products are constructed. Networking hardware and software is implemented on systems via a mechanism called network or communications architecture.

Communications architecture is the "layering" of software based upon the functionality of each layer. It is very similar to an organization chart at a corporation. At the lowest level of the protocol layers, therein lies the data link access (layer 2), the software used to talk directly to the hardware (layer 1). This is usually a very cryptic interface and very difficult to implement and maintain. In the case of Ethernet, layers 1 and 2 provide the prescribed functionality offered by Ethernet. The next layer, layer 3, is called the Network layer, although its usual function is to provide routing and transit packet support functions. At the next level (layer 4 - also called Transport) would be some sort of communications line handler whose job would be to keep messages sorted out and manage connection creation and destruction between machines. The next layer up would be a session control (layer 5) mechanism responsible for the overall message flow control and to ensure that the communication "session" between systems goes smoothly. The remainder of the upward layers (layers 6 and 7) are dedicated to direct user program interaction for specific functions. For example, one layer would be used for communications with programs desiring remote file access and manipulation, another with program-to-program communications, etc... Very few communications architectures do not use layered architectures and those that do not use layered architectures are somewhat antiquated by today's standards. The benefits of the layered approach are many, but the most significant one is the ability to change a layer's capabilities without significantly modifying the entire architecture. This feature alone makes a layered network architecture very attractive for companies desiring inter and intra systems communications capability.

As mentioned in chapter two and three, layered network architectures have their foundation in the Open Systems Interconnect (OSI) model. The OSI model has seven layers, each of which provides varying functionality as described in the previous paragraph. At each layer, there may be one or more protocols (in the case of layer 2 and above) or communications media (in the case of layer 1) that communicates with a peer protocol or media on the complementary node(s). What is means is that at any level, there can be more than one way to get data to and from the node and the only requirement is that there be the same peer at the destination node that understands what is sent.

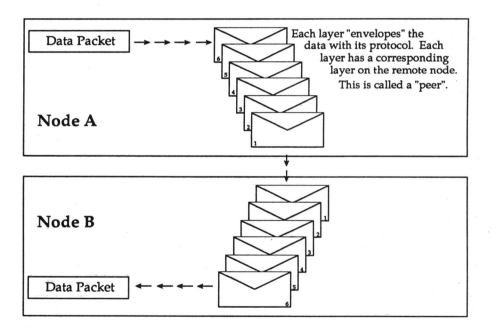

At first this may all seem a bit chaotic, and it is to an extent. It is the job of the communications architect and software/hardware engineers to put the right functionality in the right spots to keep throughput of the network high and the overhead of sending data back and forth low. If you consider each layer to have its own protocol, or filter, it is somewhat easier to understand. I tend to look at communications architectures like a glorified air purifier system. One program takes a packet of pure air and starts sending it to another program on a remote node. To insure its purity, each layer of the communications architecture puts a special container around the pure packet of air so that it will not get contaminated on the way. This means that by the time the packet of pure air is out the node, it basically has six containers around it (when it is traveling, it is in container 1, the physical layer). When the packet reaches its destination, it travels up the layers with each protocol removing the container that it knows how to remove, inspect for damage, and, if no damage is present, will send it up to the next layer. If a layer finds damage, the packet is thrown away (it's contaminated) and the source node is requested to send another pure packet of air (we can't have bad air getting to our pure air environment). This is the typical path that most data takes when using communications architectures and the layered approach.

To compound misery, communications architectures do much more than send data. Nodes (systems) need to know which nodes are available for access, which services (layers) are active, and, in some nodes, if routing is necessary. To do this, many communications architectures keep a database of active nodes, known nodes (nodes the system knows about but that may not necessarily be up and running or available), and nodes that are down. Still more, some systems on a network are known as routing nodes.

A Routing Node is a Tired Node

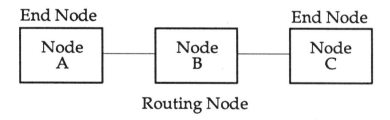

A routing node basically is a node that is very smart as to the topology of the network and how to talk to other nodes. A routing node is nothing more than a relay point. It is not magical, mystical, or hard to understand. Let's suppose that we need to go from node A to node C, but the only way to get there is through node B. In this example, A cannot "see" C, but B can. C cannot "see" A, but B can. So, since B "sees" both A and C, it is logical to presume that B can get the data from A to C. If B were a routing node, this would be possible. The packet of pure air would leave node A, travel up the architecture on node B until it hit the proper layer that handles routing functions (the layer 3 - NETWORK layer), upon which the layer would strip off its container and find that the packet does not belong on its node, but, instead, belongs on node C. Node B would then put a new container around the packet specifying node C as the destination and send the packet on its merry way. C would receive the packet and it would travel up C's protocol layers until it got to the destination program. See how simple it is? It's like leaving a message at the answering service. You call the service, leave a message and hang up. The service calls the destination (either immediately or, in some cases of store and forward, later) and delivers the message from you to the destination. Piece of cake!

Some types of communications architectures employ different schemes to implement routing capability, but the basic concept is usually the same: you send it to the routing node and it passes it on to the appropriate destination. On some networks, there may be many, many routing nodes to pass packets back and forth between destinations. In those cases, a routing node may not have direct access to the destination, but it would know which routing node would have direct access and would send the data to the next routing node in the line to get to the destination node until the data finally reached its destination. If, for some reason, there was a breakdown in communications somewhere along the path, the initiating node would be informed of the break and allowed to re-transmit the packet, or the communications path (link) would be destroyed (broken).

When considering communications on a network architecture, there is a lot more going on that immediately meets the eye. Consider the system performing routing functions for nodes on a network. That system may not have had much of a load on it before the network. Now that the network software has been installed and activated, the node will have work to do even if no data is being transmitted. When nodes are idle, they will usually send HELLO and TEST messages to each other. It's like being the Maytag re-pairman: they get lonely, so they need to communicate periodically to make sure that they are all still healthy and active. If the node being considered is a routing node, it can get beat on pretty hard even though it is not the destination for the data on the network. The "check and forward" operation that a routing node performs can drink up processor resources and cause degradation of the processor. If the processor is not very powerful, it can also degrade the network fairly substantially!

Imagine that everyone had to go to the same butcher in a small community. The butcher is capable of handling the load because he is diligent and has adequate resources to handle his clientele. Ah, but what happens when the new housing subdivision is built? Well, the butcher now gets new business that he did not have before. And, since he is the only butcher in town, he gets a lot of new business and expands his shop to handle his business. At first he can handle the new business by adding newer cutting devices, adding a room, and adding some additional personnel. His reputation grows, the community grows, his business grows. One day, however, the people start complaining about the lack of service, the long waits in line for checkout, and other delays. The butcher now has to make a decision: build a new shop or expand the new one. Well, expanding the new one may be out of the question if there is no room to expand. And building a new shop may be out of the question because of the cost and risk involved with a new shop in unknown territory or with an unstable clientele. So, the butcher can either get more work done more efficiently, expand, or add shops. Such is the quandary of routing as well: expand the routing node resources, add new routing nodes (and split up the work load), or replace the node with a completely new mechanism to handle the increased load.

A routing node is not a butcher shop, but there are many similarities. When packets have to wait to be routed, they are queued or put into a line in a holding place. Later they are de-queued and processed by the routing software and re-queued to the next layer down. The longer it take to perform this en-queueing, de-queueing, and re en-queueing is called queueing delay and is the ultimate enemy of any network. You may have the fastest communications hardware in the world. You may have the biggest IBM or DEC processor that is made on each end. But, if the traffic is routed through an IBM PC, expect the traffic to take a while to get to where it is going (for those of you who are laughing, I've seen that happen, so don't judge lest ye be judged).

Delays of the Queueing Type

Queues are everywhere on computer systems and in communications architectures, so learn to live with them. No packet of data goes straight to a device unless the engineering was done within very tight specifications and the network has a very limited usage. Most queueing of data happens in the software and usually involves multiple queues at each layer of the communications architecture. To compound the agony of delay, most operating systems impose additional queues (especially multiuser operating systems) which must be used to get data to and from its destination. The more queues an architecture has, the more the chance for bottle necks at any given queue or group of queues. Also, the overhead of processing data to and from queues will impact processor performance and, as a result, network throughput.

Now that we understand the basics of routing and queueing delay, what else is necessary to understanding network architecture? Glad you asked (isn't it amazing how you seem to ask the right questions at the right time)!?

Physical, Logical, and Error Control

There are three other basic concepts that are necessary to understanding network architecture: physical link control, logical link control, and error handling.

Physical link control usually starts happening in the transport layer of the communications architecture. The idea is to find the right physical line that is associated with the direction that the data needs to go to get to the proper remote destination. If it sounds like transport and network layers talk to each other a lot, they do! The transport layer insures that the containers sent from one node are intact when they reach the destination node. It also worries about a thing called quality of service, which is necessary to insure that the transmission linkage from A to B is good, reliable, and within specified error tolerances. The transport container contains software to provide the ability to multiplex data streams to a destination node (such as the case where multiple programs are accessing the same node on a network; no point in duplicating effort, is there?), establishing the optimum size of data packets for transmission (if the line is good, then packet sizes may be higher; if it is bad, it may need to be smaller), detecting errors in received data, checking for duplicate data packets, taking care of misdelivered packets, expediting delivery for some classes of packets (such as network control packets), and purging data when a link get zapped to expedite recovery of the network and the linkage to the remote system (if applicable).

Logical link control happens at the session layer and is the "virtual" connection between systems. The idea of session control is to allow programs requesting network access the ability to tell the network architecture "Get me to node A" without having to specify the hows and whys. Session control sets up a "session" between the programs on the nodes and feed information to the lower layers to allow the communications "session" to flow smoothly. Some vendors have set up their lower level protocols to allow multiple hardware connections between the same nodes. In this situation, the session layer would tell transport to connect node A with node B, but not which hardware device to use. If the hardware device should fail in the middle of the "session," transport layer could take action and fail over to the working hardware to the remote node. In this fashion, the "session" is kept intact and the source and destination programs never detect a break in communications at all. Session control would work with transport to make sure that the recovery was transparent to the communicating programs and communication, while slightly delayed due to the recovery, would still go on (which is the idea of a network, nicht wahr?).

Finally, error control. The concept of error control is fairly obvious: controlling and correcting errors that happen. If anyone tells you that their network is error free, ask them if they ever sold snake oil! There is no such thing. Error control is pretty simple: if any given layer of the architecture does not like the data it has been given (because of errors in formatting of data, data corruption, old data, etc.), it can send a nasty message back to the previous layer telling it that there is an error. If the previous layer can provide good data, it will. If not, it may need to go back to the previous layer to find good data and, in many cases, it may need to go back to the originator to get a good copy of the data. It is not necessary to traverse all the way up and down every layer of the architecture every time an error is found. Most of the time, errors in corrupted, duplicate, or bad data are cleared up and fixed by the time the data hits the transport layer. After that, it is usually a data formatting problem, which is more serious as it means that the remote peer protocol (the protocol at the same level as the one that detected the error) is formatting things incorrectly and will most likely require some sort of human intervention to fix the problem, and we all know what that means.

Errors can be caused by interference on the wire (electronic emission interference, magnetic interference, radio frequency interference, bulldozers cutting the wire in two, DC or AC motors next to unshielded wire, etc...), hardware problems in the communications adapters or controllers, or software bugs or other problems that cause corruption of the data between nodes. Some errors are called "intermittent" because they come and go like the the wind (and are about as hard to catch). Others are "hard" errors that can easily be tracked down (notice I didn't say easily fixed). Under most conditions with a properly functioning network architecture, errors are usually due to corrupted data packets due to line synchronization failures, packet collisions, and other such items.

Network Software Selection

Now that we have a thorough understanding of the issues of network architectures, what criteria can be imposed upon the selection of software to solve the network problem on Ethernet?

There are quite a few software packages that run on Ethernet and even more coming out each day. Which one is best for a particular applications depends greatly on the application. Another issue is that of the architecture of the network selected and how it applies to the Ethernet technology.

One major computer vendor recently tried to get their architecture to work on the Ethernet. Since Ethernet is a broadcast-oriented technology and also tends to work well with network architectures that do not require a "master" node, the implementation of the network architecture in the Ethernet environment was less than satisfactory. The network architecture was a circuit-oriented architecture with a hierarchical structure, meaning that nodes wishing to connect to each other must go through a central control node. Because of the overhead associated with such actions, the usage of Ethernet as a transport medium caused some serious throughput problems, especially on the central node and the network implementation was abandoned in favor of a network plan that fit well into the Ethernet environment.

What does all of this mean? Simply that the network architecture selected to solve a particular problem needs not only to allow the desired connectivity and control, but also needs the performance necessary for the application. Frequently good network architectures that work well with leased lines and packet switched networks (and other WAN technologies) do not work well with LAN technologies. Some companies have resorted to providing specialized protocols and handling schemes for LAN-oriented network implementations in a particular architecture.

In most cases, just because a network architecture works well with various types of network technologies does not mean that the network architecture will work well in the Ethernet environment or any other LAN environment. A decision to implement a network architecture over Ethernet should be carefully considered on the part of the vendor, but many customers desirous of Ethernet access push vendors into implementations of popular architectures before considering the ramifications. Architectures that use a hierarchical structure or those that are heavily circuit-oriented (connection-oriented) can cause undue overhead on an Ethernet and provide poor performance even though the hardware and technology is capable of much greater capabilities.

Some network architectures actually use various protocols and access techniques to provide the necessary connectivity and services across various network architectures. DECnet, for instance, utilizes the Digital Data Communications Message Protocol (DDCMP) as the base-level protocol for most of its communications mechanisms. In cases, however, where another base level protocol is more functional, it is used as in the case of X.25. Further still, some features of DECnet provide the ability to use a protocol such as Maintenance Operations Protocol (MOP) to support features such as loopback testing, downline system loading, and other functions best served by a specific protocol. In all cases, a network architecture in the LAN environment should provide for optimal utilization of the environment regardless of the original or current environments supported.

Chapter Summary

Network architecture is nothing more than a tiered or layered approach to the implementation of the communications mechanism between nodes. Some architectures follow the seven-layer OSI model, some do not. It does not make one better than another, but it can make each more difficult to understand or to get the dissimilar architectures to work with each other. Just because a network architecture conforms to the OSI architecture **DOES NOT MEAN THAT IT IS COMPATIBLE WITH OTHER OSI IMPLEMEN-TATIONS BY OTHER VENDORS**. That is akin to saying that all implementations of BASIC on different systems are the same. Hogwash! Just as with languages, network architectures can be radically different and must be carefully chosen for your environment.

Your biggest enemy in the communications world is queueing delay. Queueing delay is an elusive thing and difficult to measure (a Ph.D. in statistics helps, but not much), but is there and can be estimated. Remember that all network architectures impose queueing delays upon your data while it is in transit and should be monitored closely.

Finally, remember that processors not currently running communications software will be degraded when running communications software. More work is imposed upon the processor and more resources need to be used. In some situations, the communications architecture implemented on the system is more sophisticated than the operating system itself and requires more resources (sad, but very true in a great many instances). Plan for the degradation, choose routing nodes carefully, and always be mindful of queueing delay.

To quote an old Doonesbury saying by Uncle Duke:

"Be firm, fly low, and stay cool."

Chapter Seven

Designing An Ethernet

The most savage controversies are those about matters as to which there is no good evidence either way.

Bertrand Russell

Introduction

Once you have selected Ethernet as an appropriate network for your communications needs, the next step is the design cycle. Designing a LAN is a lot more involved than it seems and it begins with the network design.

Network Design and Analysis

Network design and analysis is a term we networking types apply to the basic methods necessary to PROPERLY design a network. A properly generated network design can provide a company with the following benefits:

o Proper analysis of existing equipment for network installation
o List of requirements for network installation
o Proper configuration of network components for optimum cost savings
o A network topology that is flexible and adaptable
o Correct selection of network hardware for the network function
o Correct selection of network software for the network function
o Documentation of the network for future enhancements and modifications
o Migration path into future network technologies without re-design
o A long network life-cycle (reducing the costs of potential replacement)
o Interconnect paths and methods for multiple network architectures
o User analysis and configuration of network resources for optimal use
o Network management plan and methodology to reduce downtime and allow for maximum use of available resources
o Expectations for performance, reliability, and usability
o Optimal programming environment for network(ed) applications
o Training needs for programmers, users, and network managers
o Recurring expense forecasting and budgeting methods
o Network support needs (programming, management, user support)
o Use of mathematical modeling tools to help insure the success of the network design and topology
o Optimal design to prevent network congestion, queueing delay, and proper placement of routing and management resources on the network

Take a hard look at the above list and ask yourself if your network design encompasses all the above issues and needs. Then ask yourself if you have adequately considered this list of items. If you have, super! If you have not, you haven't properly designed your network.

Network design is much more than ordering the parts and pieces from a vendor. It is much more than the suggestions the vendor gives you for configuration of your network. As a potential user of network components, you have the final decision on any network configuration and no matter what the vendor tells you to buy, the final decision to buy rests upon your shoulders. If the network doesn't work as promoted to management, you can blame the vendor, but the ultimate person responsible is you - the person who recommended to management the network components to buy. And, if you think for one second that the smiling vendor across the desk from you is going to recommend some other vendor than himself for your network, you are either naive or you have been listening to too much vendor hype ("We're not here to make money we're here to be your friend!"). So, remember, the person that will catch the blame from your company in the end is not the vendor–it's you! If you want to exercise implicit trust your vendor, great. There are few people that are qualified network designers and you can bet that you are not going to get access to them from a vendor for free. Remember - you get what you pay for.

The first step of network design is identification of the need for a network. While this may seem obvious, few companies sit down and spend some time logically defining the reasons for installing a network. Going through this exercise tells you whether or not a network is necessary to accomplish the desired function, or whether there is a more cost-effective method to solve the problem at hand. I was asked to design a network for a large financial company one time and after looking over the needs very carefully, I told them that they didn't need a network. At first, the management of the company thought that I was nuts because their vendor had been hammering on them for months that they needed a network. They simply took it for gospel that they needed one and eventually the vendor got to the upper management and convinced them that they needed a network to solve their "problems." I was called in because the customer didn't know anything about networking and did not have the ultimate confidence in the vendor's efforts to find the "right" solution, regardless of what the vendor solutions were. After working on the project for three weeks, I found that the methodology adopted by the company's management for distributing workload and the reporting hierarchy involved was functioning very well and there was less than 5% out-flow of work to other company entities. What this meant was that 95% of the work being done in the respective branches stayed within the branch and did not require corporate intervention to get work accomplished. Also, all work was done in a reasonable manner and placing a computer in the middle of the paperwork effort would do nothing but slow things down (yes, Virginia, computers are not always better). I went back to the customer's management and explained all of this to them and they immediately called the vendor and demanded an explanation. The vendor told them I was wrong and proceeded to do the one thing that a vendor should never do–cut down the competition. Since I was their "competition," it was obvious to them that I was trying to deprive them of a sale, and they felt that they were right and I was wrong. Now I was mad! I spent another two weeks (at the customer's request) thoroughly documenting the lack of need for the network and also fighting some of the irrational claims of the vendor (I asked the vendor once why it was that they were pushing the network so hard when the customer didn't need it; their answer was "Because."). At the end, the vendor backed off their claims as the vendor had not done a thorough (or even partial) job of looking at the customer's needs and how the customer conducted business. The vendor had no idea as to what the customer's plans were for the next fiscal year, nor did the vendor bother to look into the budgetary constraints that the customer was under. All the vendor cared about was making the sale no matter how much the customer did not need it or how much it cost. The entire hassle could have been avoided if the customer had thought, carefully, about why they "needed" a network. Instead, the customer was heavily influenced by the vendor's sales tactics and got swept up in the buying frenzy that usually accompanies a great many sales of networks. Also, the customer should have looked first to the company business plan. It would have told them whether a network was necessary to achieve the business goals of the company or not, based upon expected market penetration, growth factors, profitability requirements, and personnel requirements. So, rule number one is make sure that you need a network; don't go out and buy one due to unjustified internal pressure, vendor pressure, or peer pressure (yes, we all wish that we had a network just like company X down the street).

Rule Number Two

After a need for a network has been established, rule number two in network design is applied: what is it supposed to do and how much is it going to cost? What it is supposed to do is a matter of defining, very carefully, what functionality the network is to offer. If it is electronic mail, file transfer, or task-to-task communications, great, but WRITE IT DOWN! Also, keep the base functionality of the network clear, concise, and simple. Too many good intentions get shot down because the base rationale was too complex for technical personnel to understand, much less the management personnel who have to approve and budget for it. Remember that your company's management is the signing authority for technical purchases and direction, regardless of what you have been told. If they can't understand what the needs are, you can bet that they will be more than a little apprehensive about installing technology they do not understand. I once told a company that a network does nothing and then explained that if it did anything at all, they should be glad. Setting expectations is very important and this is accomplished by carefully defining the network functionality.

Network Costing

So far, identification of need and identification of functionality have been defined. Now comes the problem of cost. Networks are just like systems in many ways: they have a life cycle, they require periodic upgrading and expansion, there are recurring costs such as software and hardware maintenance, telco service, packet services, modems, etc., they require personnel to manage and maintain the network components, software may need to be developed so there may be costs for software engineering or applications programming, etc... The point is this: if you think that because network components are less expensive than a given system, think again. The overall cost of services and expansion will show that over a period of time, the network may turn out to be the most costly portion of your overall computing plan. Why? Simple. Networks, for all the high-tech bruhaha they have generated, are very expensive to install and operate over a period of time because they are "service-intensive." What this refers to is the fact that networks require the use of vendor services more than a typical computer system might due to their inherent complexity and lack of a wide understanding of network technology by users, programmers, and managers. Networks are used for communications, and communications services are expensive. Yes, networks can save a company a lot of money **IF THEY ARE USED CONSISTENTLY AND PROPERLY.** The sad thing is that without proper design, neither consistency or proper use of a network is achieved by most network users. To illustrate how expenses can creep up on you, here are some things that affect the cost of networking:

1. Cost of hardware components (modems, cabling, channel interfaces, controllers, cabinetry, protocol converters, line conditioners, protocol analyzers, time domain reflectometers, frequency spectrum analyzers, breakout boxes, bit error rate testers, multiplexers, packet assembler/disassembler boxes, traffic analyzers response time analyzers, phone set tester, line testers, manual and automatic switching units, autodialers, protocol simulators, converters, data encryption equipment, auto callback units, data compression units, junction panels, line drivers, protocol converters, repeaters, bridges, voice frequency testers, front-end processors, servers, and many others)

2. Cost of software components (networking architecture packages (such as DECnet, SNA, TCP/IP, and others), protocol emulators, protocol conversion, data compression, data analysis, network management, network troubleshooting, network statistics, network security, network applications (such as electronic mail, distributed database applications, office systems, etc...), operating system interfacing software, etc...)

3. Cost of operational services (leased-line cost, building conduit space costs, packet-switch network hookups, packet-switched network kilopacket charges, equipment leases, cable installation and add-ons, earth station channel charges, transponder channel charges, dial-up charges (digital service), dial-up charges (analog service), service surcharges for exceeding pre-agreed usage levels of shared services, general equipment maintenance, software maintenance, pickup/delivery and destination charges, line conditioning, per-call maintenance, per-call consulting services, administrative charges, etc...)

4. Cost of consulting (network design, data collection, data reduction and analysis, network topology, traffic matrix, routing matrix, performance models, applications design, applications programming, queueing delay analysis, network technology assessment, network implementation, network installation, network management, network user training, network programmer training, network manager training, network project management, network troubleshooting and fault finding, network enhancements and add-ons, network interconnect design and implementation, interconnect training, network planning, network facilities survey, and many more)

5. Cost of replacement due to improper initial design (all of the above plus the original cost to implement the current network)

While this may look like an extensive list, it isn't. That means that there are plenty of other costs that can come out of nowhere that were not expected or not properly planned for. You may look at this list and say to yourself that you don't need all the stuff listed above. This may be true, but I feel that with the influx of network technology and the price of the hardware dropping, you will find yourself involved in networking in the near future if you are not already involved. This also means that although you may not use some of the equipment and components listed above, what's to say that you will not later on in your current company or in some other computing life? By the way, for all you MicroVAX buyers out there, do you honestly think that you can do without an Ethernet between them for too long? Digital doesn't think so. For all you companies buying MV's and not thinking about networking them, dream on. Many companies that I deal with are just now starting to see the problem of purchasing MV's. It's not the cost of the hardware or the functionality (which are superb, by the way) its the distributed management, support, and logistics costs that kill you.

Rule Number Three - The Site Survey

Now that we have identified a need for a network, we know what it is supposed to do, and we know that there are a lot of things that can affect the cost, the next thing to do is rule number three of network design: the site survey.

The site survey is not a trivial thing. Site surveys involve the careful examination of company facilities, building architecture, phone facilities (if you are using phone lines), existing computer hardware and software components, examination of existing contracts (to see if some already cover the needs for the network), power facilities, HVAC facilities, wireways and wire centers, electromagnetic interference possibilities, radio frequency interference possibilities, safety issues, security issues, building wiring and fire codes, electrical codes, reception and shipping facilities, building maintenance capabilities, on-site or vendor maintenance capabilities, and other related items. While this may initially seem to be not necessary, consider what happened to a designer when he was designing the cable layout for a large multinational company. He carefully measured the cable length needs and used a building diagram given to him by the customer as the basis for layout of the wire plan. What he did not know was that he was using an old plan and that many of the walls and wireways had changed. As a result, he planned a wire run directly through the new cafeteria, which was not on the building diagram. Fortunately, since a proper site survey involves the customer, software, hardware, sales, service, and other selected personnel, the mis-layout of the wire plan was caught before the plan was finalized, and corrections were made. Site surveys involve many people and require quite a bit of time to properly lay out the network in the environment in which it will function and to insure that all the "players" are where they are supposed to be when they are supposed to be there to insure a smooth installation of the network.

Rule Number Four

Rule number four is the basic network design, data collection/reduction, and data analysis. Network design, as I said before, is not as simple as throwing the wire down, hooking it up, and tossing some software on the machine. Network design is a science that has grown quite complicated as more and more sophisticated networks have evolved. A network designer starts out by actively and aggressively investigating all the needs, wants, hopes, and aspirations for the network that a company wishes to implement. He then takes the justifications that a company has written up, the functionality statement, and the site survey and identifies missing parts and pieces necessary to the network design. Following collection of data to satisfy the parts and pieces that are missing, the designer sets out to investigate the proper type of technology that the company requires now and to achieve their future goals for the network. Isolation of the proper technology is a critical step in solid network design. By providing alternative technologies, the network designer can give the customer a few good options by which to implement the network, which can result in time and cost savings as well as reducing the risk of a single network technology causing network failures due to flaws, bugs, or other problems.

Modeling Tools

Once a series of technologies have been defined, the designer then uses mathematical modeling tools (manual and computer-based) to figure out data flow ratios, probabilities of error, queueing delays, interconnect problems, least-cost network topological layout, routing paths, redundancy paths, and many more necessary items essential to solid network design. The modeled data is collected and reduced to meaningful facts and figures about the design and compared to network requirements dictated by the customer. If the results fit the requirements window, the network design being analyzed may be useful in the customer's environment (provided it meets physical needs, support needs, etc.). This process is repeated for every reasonable network technology until all the potential technologies are completely modeled. Following the modeling of network data, a financial analysis is done to determine how much the network is going to cost to implement, start-up, maintain, and expand. This is another exhaustive analysis that requires thought on the future of the network as well as applying practical experience with the theoretical network model. Finally, an assessment analysis is performed to identify networks that are "most" useful (closest to the desired functionality) and "least" useful (on the right track, but not closest to the desired combination of price/performance/ease of use, etc...). Once all of these items have been done, the network designer takes the results back to the site survey team and works with them to iron out any particular problems with the network designs as well as help isolate which design best suits the needs of the customer.

Human Issues

Another document the network designer will typically generate is one defining personnel needs and operational considerations. This document typically describes the type of personnel necessary to get the job done and what kind of personnel will be necessary for the day-to-day support of the network and its related components. In addition to the base personnel needs, a breakdown of costing for such personnel might also be included.

Formal Design Documentation

Once a particular network design has been identified by the network designer and the site survey team, a formal design document is drafted. It documents the rationale for the design, a description of the components, a network topology, a wiring diagram, expansion capabilities, expected life cycle, applications support environment (and package descriptions, if applicable), network management environment, potential problems, data throughput analysis, testing and verification procedures, identification of network installation resources, an implementation timetable, personnel and training needs, cost analysis, and risks. The formal design document is the backbone to the network design and serves as a guideline for implementation and expansion. Following generation of the design document, a presentation is also created for the customer's management so that all parties involved thoroughly understand what the network looks like, what it is capable of doing, what resources are required, how long it will take to implement it and how much it will cost to implement, support, and maintain.

By now you have probably realized that there is not a network in place yet, and still there have been quite a few people involved and an obvious amount of work has been done. Why go through all this grief just for a network?

The Reason for Design and Analysis

The answer is simple and yet complex (the yin and yang of networks): proper business procedure and reduction of potential risks. I had a management friend of mine come up to me once and asked me why all of this was necessary for the sake of installing a wire, some controllers, and some software. I told him that it is like playing the stock market. There are people who buy a stock because it "looks" good; they may not have qualified the prospect, but they have a good feeling about it, so they buy the stock. This is the "gut feel" approach. Sometimes it works, sometimes it doesn't, but studies have proven that it does not work more often than not (about 78% failures). Granted, there are some that seem to know how to use the gut feel approach very well and are very good at it, but these people are very few and far between. The second type try to play the stock market on their own. They read up on it for a while, read some analysis work on given stock types, and proceed to use a discount broker to invest their money in stocks that they select. This approach is usually not successful for a very long time due to the long learning curve necessary to play the stock game and the need to watch stocks over a pretty fair piece of time. The self-broker stock player is usually dismally profitable at first and may improve later on if he does not get frustrated and quit first. The third type of stock player is the high-risk options player. This type can be a gambler type and can make a killing or go bust within a day. Options players have to really understand the market to play well and profit. The fourth type is the stock player that uses a broker to invest his money in stocks in hopes that the broker can pick the right stocks and make the right decisions to generate a profit for the stock player. This is somewhat akin to using a consultant: there are very, very good stock brokers, but there are a lot of mediocre or poor stock brokers who are not overly cautious with their customer's investments and can ruin potentially reasonable deals. The final type of stock player is one who is a stock expert and can play the game himself with confidence due to his in-depth and expert understanding of the stock market. I then told my friend that most people are very leery about playing the stocks by themselves. I asked him how many options players he knew and how many expert stock players he knew. He answered that he didn't know any. Most people interested in the stock market try to find a good broker and the amount they pay the broker is worth it for the lower risk they are taking, the lack of need to become a "guru" in the stock market methodology, not to mention the reduction in time that it takes to monitor their investment.

When looking at network design and analysis, the main mistake that many companies make is that they approach a network in the same manner that they might approach the self-broker methodology. Nothing could be worse. Networks have some fairly serious restrictions on them that many systems do not. There are many more systems "experts" than there are network "experts" due to the complexity of network design as well as the lack of general network design education and information. Most systems have training and documents available for learning the hows and whys of systems hardware and software. Networks, unfortunately, are subject to the whims of multiple types of systems trying to talk to one another, frequently on differing technology, and takes on dimensions that most systems never have to worry about. Compound that with a severe lack of good, clear user documentation, technology information, and design documentation, and network designers capable of designing superior networks are few and far between and usually rely on heavy experience and learning networking "the hard way."

Chapter Summary

If you have been scared to death about network design and analysis as a result of reading this chapter, good! It also means that you may now realize that the proper design of a network is critical to making the network cost effective over the long run, as well as understanding that just because you have sharp systems people, they may not be able to design a network properly due to lack of information and experience.

Using consultants in the network design phase can help drastically reduce the risk factor of the network, and a good consultant can tell you what he can do and what you can do. This will save money in the short and long term, as well as provide you a solid network design. While it is true that you can design your network yourself, it is not necessarily true that the network will survive over the long haul, nor can you feel comfortable that it will perform as expected if you have not done a performance analysis before the network is in place. Proper network design can save a ton of money down the road and is cost-effective up-front if done correctly. If you are penny-wise and dollar-foolish, you will, indeed, end up paying more, later.

The next time you look at designing a network for your company or your friend, go down the list of benefits at the beginning of this chapter and ask yourself if you have received all of them. If not, you may have missed something somewhere. If you can claim that you have them all, you have benefitted from a good network design and can expect years of cost-effective service from your network.

Chapter Eight

A Sample Installation

The essence of success is that it is never necessary to think of a new idea oneself. It is far better to wait until somebody else does it, and then to copy him in every detail, except his mistakes.

Aubrey Menen

Introduction

As an example, let's consider the installation of a small Ethernet LAN. For the purposes of discussion, here is a recap of Ethernet's specifications for configuration and use:

Speed: 10Mbit/sec
Data Transmission Type: Digital, Manchester encoded
Maximum number of nodes per segment: 100
Maximum length of a single thick segment: 500 meters
Total number of nodes per total Ethernet: 1024
Maximum separation between nodes: 2.8 Kilometers
Protocol used: Carrier Sense Multiple Access with Collision Detect (CSMA/CD)
Distance between individual node connections: 2.5 meters
Thick Cable type: Shielded coax
Packet size: 64 to 1518 bytes
Connection Mechanism: Non-intrusive cable tap

For the sake of argument, we will presume that the proper network analysis and design has been done and Ethernet was the choice made. We will also presume that the network has two nodes and that the nodes are physically 10 feet apart to keep things simple.

Installation Steps

In our installation, please keep in mind that the LAN could easily be a token ring, token bus, or any other LAN for that matter. There are certain nuances particular to Ethernet, but these are few. LAN installation requires certain steps to be taken to insure success and these are common across all LAN architectures. Installation steps for successful installations include:

1. Preparation of the site
2. Cable testing and installation

3. Preparation of the cable for installation of taps and transceivers
4. Installation of taps and transceivers
5. Installation of bulkhead wire assemblies on host processors
6. Host processor preparation for installation of network controller
7. Installation of network controller
8. Diagnostic checkout of installed components
9. Adjustment of system parameters for communications hardware and software
10. Installation of communications software
11. Configuration of the network database
12. Activation of the network software
13. Testing of network software/hardware
14. Throughput analysis
15. User training
16. Turnover for use

In the following sections, we will examine each of the steps involved in the installation of the Ethernet product on a generic basis. While there are nuances to any product, the important concept to grasp is the steps necessary to install a LAN, not necessarily which one.

1. Preparation of the Site

Site preparation involves the readying of the location where the LAN will be installed. In many places, the biggest problem in the installation is the placement of the cable for the network.

Most office buildings have electrical ducts called wireways or wiretrays. In these ducts all the electrical wiring for the building is placed and it usually runs down the length of most halls or in a grid-like fashion above the main areas of the building. Wireways are also set up to run between floors of a building through the elevator shaft or through strategically- placed holes between floors (usually in closets that contain all the telephone equipment and punch-down blocks). In many sites, the LAN cable will be run down the wireway with the other cables. This is where most troubles begin.

If the computers are located in the same room, the location of the LAN cable is usually not a big deal. If there is raised flooring, the cable can be run under the floor. If there is no raised flooring, the cable can be run above floor as long as it is protected from human interference (such as stepping on it, kicking, running things over it, etc...). In areas where an entire floor may have a LAN, it is necessary to install LAN cable throughout the area of usage. In our example, we will concern ourselves with the installation between systems and not the problems of floor-wide LAN cabling. Suffice it to say for now that caution must be exercised when installing cable in wireways due to their inconvenient locations (at times), other cables, and frequent access by electricians and other individuals not associated or knowledgeable about LANs.

In our situation, we will presume the cable to be run under the floor. But, how much cable is necessary?

We know from our specification that the systems are 10 feet apart. We also know that rise distance will most likely be no more than 6 feet above the floor (most computer cabinets are not taller than that) and that we should allow for about 2 foot slack on each end. Add that up and we come to 26 feet of cable. Now, to compound the problem slightly, we know that nodes cannot be closer than 2.5 meters (approx 8.2 feet). That means that we can tap in three places in the 26 foot segment of Ethernet cable (we only need two places). If we take the measurements from one end, the first tap would be at 8.2 feet, the second at 16.4 and the third at 24.6. While the third tap does not pose much of a problem, the first one might as it will be 8.2 feet from the end of the cable and that would be under the floor of the computer room. And you thought LAN cabling was simple.

Not to worry. In Ethernet, we have a situation which can help us. Ethernet cabling consists of three cable segments per node that allow a single node to tap in to the Ethernet cable itself. These are:

1. Cable from the controller to the cabinet external cable connector
2. Cable from the external connector to the transceiver unit
3. Ethernet cable itself to which the transceiver directly connects

Most vendors allow the customer to order differing lengths of cable for each segment. Do not get the tapping segmentation confused with Ethernet cable segments. Tapping segmentation is included as part of the method to get on to the Ethernet cable. Ethernet segmentation is taking the Ethernet cable itself and cutting it into separate Ethernet segments.

Therefore, our cabling needs for two nodes are:

o Two (2) controller cables 5 feet long
o Two (2) transceiver cables 10 feet long
o One (1) Ethernet segment 25 feet long

This cabling configuration will provide a minimum cable configuration for our Ethernet network needs.

Following identification of cable lengths, we need to plan for the installation of the cable, the controller, and the software. While all that happens later, part of the site preparation is getting all the parties together and getting decisions made to get the LAN in place correctly the first time.

2. Cable Testing and Installation

Once the cable has arrived, it needs to be tested BEFORE it is installed. In larger LAN installations, it is wise to test the cable while it is still on the reel to insure that the reel of cable is still good. A simple test can be done with a Ohmmeter (a baseband cable should read between 48 and 52 ohms) but a better method is to use a device called a Time Domain Reflectometer (TDR). The purpose of a TDR is to send electrical pulses down the wire and test for how long it takes the pulses to return. If the pulses take an infinite amount of time, the cable is flawless (electrically) and should work fine. If the TDR says that the cable is 10 meters long, you can bet that there is a break about 10 meters down or there is a short of some kind. In those cases where fiber is used, there is a device called a Fiber Optic TDR (FOTDR or OTDR) that gives the same type of capabilities as a coaxial or other copper cable TDR. Some TDRs allow the user to get a hard copy printout of the cable wave form. This can be very useful in secure environments where it is important to know the number of nodes on the cable, how far apart they are, and if any nodes have been added since the last test. I usually use a TDR to show the cable pullers that the cable is good and that it had best be good when they finish pulling the cable through the wireways. By the way, the common term for this is called "ringing out the wire." After the cable has been pulled, it is a good idea to test the cable again with the TDR to insure that the cable is solid and there are no shorts or breaks.

3. Preparation of the Cable for Installation of Taps and transceivers

Most LANs connect nodes to the main LAN cable through devices called transceivers (transmitter/receiver). The idea of a transceiver is very simple: it transmits electrical signals to the main LAN wire and receives electrical signals from the main LAN wire and passes them back to the controller. transceivers are hooked on to the main LAN cable through a connection called a tap. Taps come in two flavors: intrusive and non-intrusive. Intrusive taps are those that cause the cable to be disrupted, totally, while the tap is being installed. A non-intrusive tap does not disrupt any other operations on the cable while the installation is being done. Another benefit of the non-intrusive mechanism is the reduction of active connections on the cable. If the cable is not broken up, there are fewer places for it to fail or to act like an antenna for radio or electrical signals (connectors will do that). In the case of Ethernet, the type of tap used depends entirely upon the vendor. The specification calls for non-intrusive types of taps, but that is not always practical or practiced by vendors. In the case of fiber optics, practically all tapping mechanisms are the intrusive type, but with the use of new selective-light amplification tapping units and transceivers, companies are starting to introduce non-intrusive tap mechanisms for fiber optic cable plants. Installing a tap on a cable, such as Ethernet, requires a tapping tool of some sort and a flashlight. Tapping tools are usually a manual operation (utilizing a clamp for the cable, an alignment guide, and a screw-in tool that will eat away the shielding and appropriate dielectric at the appropriate depths), but some utilize a drill bit with a battery-powered drill. Many people opt to buy the drill themselves, but, UNDER NO CIRCUMSTANCES, should an AC powered drill be used. If used, the AC powered drill can cause a ground loop throughout the coaxial cable, effectively shorting every transceiver hooked up to the cable. Since some transceivers can cost up to $700.00 each, such a mistake can get very expensive in a big hurry! Use the battery-powered drill and keep the cable happy. Once the hole is made by the drill or the tapping tool, use the flashlight to remove any leftover dielectric, shielding, or braid that may potentially cause static or a short.

Once the tap is ready, it is time to install the transceiver. Transceivers come in various shapes, sizes, and prices, but it is CRITICAL that the appropriate transceiver be used with the correct network controller (on the CPU side) and with the correct cable diameter (on the Ethernet cable side). Most vendor will only support LAN connections with their own hardware all the way to the Ethernet cable. Mixing or matching to save money will do nothing but cause very large support problems in the future, not to mention a lot of finger pointing. The cable diameter is important, as most transceivers for LANs have a cable guide of a pre-defined size for a pre-defined cable diameter. If the cable is too large in diameter, the tap for the transceiver (a spine-like protrusion that connects the transceiver to the cable) may not reach the center coaxial conductor. If the cable diameter is too small, the spine may overshoot the center conductor or, worse, cause a cable short by connecting to the shielding or braid on the other side of the center conductor.

Attaching transceivers to the cable is usually pretty simple. Most vendors use an allen-wrench set-up that allows the transceiver to be screwed down into position with few problems. Also, most transceivers have alignment clamps and guides built into the transceiver housing, so it is fairly straightforward to get a transceiver on to a cable.

Once the transceiver is connected to the cable, the transceiver cable is attached. This operation involves the use of the cable that runs from the computer cabinet bulkhead to the transceiver itself. Most transceiver cables use a 9– or 12-pin "D" connector, which is screwed in using a small screwdriver (similar to the way that terminals are attached to EIA-232D cables) or uses a sliding lock mechanism. When the transceiver cable is installed, use a plastic cable tie (you can get them from any electronic shop, or ask your field service engineer—they usually have a ton of them) to connect the hanging transceiver cable to a secure place on the transceiver and another cable tie to secure the bulkhead connection end of the cable to the bulkhead. This will reduce the strain on the connectors and keep an accidental pull of the transceiver cable from ripping apart connectors or causing a fault that is hard to track down (due to the cable being partially connected, etc.).

5. Installation of Bulkhead Wire Assemblies on Host Processor(s)

This step is fairly easy. Most LAN cabling systems use an interconnection point that allows the controller cable to be connected to the transceiver cable. Such interconnects are nothing but a passive (no power) connector block that takes one cable format and converts it to another cable format (such as ribbon cable to 12-wire round cable). Bulkhead wire assemblies are usually attached to the inside open space of a peripheral cabinet, close to the location where the network interface board is located. Installation usually requires a screwdriver and a wrench to tighten any nuts that may be used to secure the adapter to the cabinet.

6. Host Processor Preparation for Installation of Network Controller

On many systems, the installation of new hardware controllers is fairly straightforward. Some network controllers, however, require backplane re-wiring or adaptation (such as in the case of direct memory access options on some computer busses) as well as special power supplies due to power loading factors. Your network vendor can give you specifications that are necessary for power, cooling, installation operations, and other requirements that your field service engineer may need to install the device. You will also need to insure that there is sufficient, open backplane space that will allow the installation of the network controller. If there is not, it may be necessary to install additional backplane space and that can get very expensive. If your system is a small, well marked machine such as the IBM PC (and compatibles), the IBM System 36, and others, it may be possible to do the hardware installation yourself. In most cases, however, don't get your hopes up too high, as the vendor will most likely need to install the device.

On some systems, devices require a unique system bus address that is usually switch-selectable by the field service engineer during installation. That address is what is used to interrupt the processor during I/O operations and is usually referenced in any driver software that is used to allow the hardware to communicate with the system. As a result, changing the hardware addressing may cause failure of the software. Care must be exercised to make sure that both the hardware and the software addressing is set up for the same address(es). While on the subject of addressing, network components almost always have a network address as well. On some networking architectures, the network address is set in software; on others, it is in hardware. It is very important to find out IN ADVANCE which mechanism your network will use and assign addresses to nodes prior to network hardware installation. Many vendors send their boards pre-set to a factory address; if all the systems are simply "plugged-in" and the addresses are all the same on all nodes, you can imagine the chaotic response that can happen. So, there will usually be a system bus address and a network address, but they are not the same and will usually require some forethought for both.

In addition to the hardware requirements, there are software goodies to think about as well. Most systems will require the system to be modified to allow the new controller to work properly as well as driver software installed to allow the new controller to work with the operating system. System modifications are usually in the form of a system generation (SYSGEN) which causes the entire system to be re-built for the new configuration. On some larger systems, this is a major ordeal and can cause a variety of problems for already functioning components and software. For other systems, a SYSGEN takes, literally, seconds and does not disturb most applications or components. The safest way to prepare for the installation is to presume the worst and hope for the best. That way you are never disappointed. Presume that it will take a while to get the host operating system in shape to talk to the network controller and that the installation will be a major ordeal, as it usually turns out to be anyway.

7. Installation of the Network Controller Hardware

If the system has been prepared properly, the installation of the network controller is not that painful. A checklist should have been established for installation and other customers contacted to verify the suppositions that have been made about the installation. Once the hardware has been installed, it usually will have on-board diagnostics in the hardware that can be invoked through a switch command on the board or through a software utility. Always check out the hardware to make sure that it says that everything is OK. Many LAN controllers have LEDs that allow the user to see if there is a failure or if everything is functioning properly. Check your manuals to see how to make use of the LEDs and what they mean; it can save you a bunch of time later on when the network component fails.

If the Ethernet controller is for a PC, be sure to check to see if the proper DIP switches have been set for the transceiver to either be enabled or disabled on the card. Typically, the transceiver will be enabled if the controller is to be attached to a thinwire (RG58) coax or to an unshielded twisted pair. If the controller is to be connected to a thickwire, the transceiver will typically be disabled on the controller as the controller will be connected to a transceiver that is connected directly to the thickwire cable.

8. Diagnostic Checkout of Installed Components

The golden rule of diagnostics, known as Bill's Law of Diagnostics, is as follows:

"Diagnostics are software and are subject to fail at any time. They also tend to lie. Often."

This means that you, too, can be confused and amazed by what seems like properly functioning hardware ("The diagnostics say everything is fine") which, in reality, is highly broke. The Corollary to Bill's Law of Diagnostics is:

"Different versions of diagnostics lie differently."

So, diagnostics are only as good as the software engineer who wrote them. Some versions will work better than others, so if you do not like the results from one set of diagnostics, you can most likely try another set and get a different result. And, since most diagnostics are not written by the hardware engineers that built the hardware, you can imagine some of the things that can happen.

Be very wary of new diagnostics. As with any program, diagnostics will have bugs and flaws that will be corrected over a period of time. Like other programs, they are constantly under upgrades or revisions and will have certain versions that will work better than others and some versions without the proper support for the necessary option that you bought for the network.

Diagnostics can be very helpful in tracking down a problem with the network hardware. Some vendors even supply a diagnostic routine that runs on every node and allows the diagnostics on the various nodes to perform a node-to-node checkout of the hardware path (this is one of the best methods of checkout besides the actual communications package being active and working properly). Before you install your hardware, check with other users of the network, and ask for their opinion on diagnostics and other troubleshooting tools. Some network technologies are very good; others leave much to be desired. Your risk is reduced when you know the facts up front.

For the sake of argument, we will presume that the diagnostics work correctly. During the installation, the diagnostics show that there is a fault with the network component and the installation engineer decides that a replacement is necessary. When purchasing the network components, you should have specified a maintenance contract with the vendor. Now is the time to see how well the vendor responds to the problem. Many times, the installer can get another board in 24 hours. In some situations, the vendor will require that the board be returned before another is shipped out. In still other situations, the board will need to be sent out, repaired, and then returned. In all situations, a board will most likely be swapped and will require re-configuration of the system, temporarily, to overlook the bad board or to configure it out of the system while the replacement is being shipped in.

Board replacement is a funny thing. In most companies, when you buy a component, you are shipped a new board. When the board fails (and it will—it's just a matter of how long before it does), it is usually swapped for a functional board. Did you just put in a new board again? Most likely not. You will probably get a "factory re-furbished" board, not a new one. That means that the board was used at some other site, failed, and has been fixed and re-tested to meet quality assurance standards. Does that mean that the replacement component is subject to failure? You bet. Does it mean that it will fail quicker than the new board? Not necessarily. A lot depends upon the vendor quality assurance program and the methods used to verify fixed components. Don't panic because you get a used replacement. After all, you are giving the vendor a used board anyway. Do be concerned over the vendor's quality assurance mechanism and check it out before you need it.

9. Adjustment of System Parameters for Communications Hardware and Software

After the hardware is installed and checked out properly, it is usually necessary to modify the system parameters to allow the hardware to be recognized properly and to allow the software drivers to be properly configured into the system. The vendor will usually provide guidelines for this and one of the requirements may involve a SYSGEN (discussed previously). Exercise care with this step and there should be few problems getting the components to be recognized by the system.

10. Installation of the Communications Software

While it is true that it looks like we have already taken care of the communications hardware, it is possible that the vendor provides standalone network interfaces that need to be installed after the host controller is installed and functional. Not all LANs are alike and some have some rather bizarre configurations to be implemented.

Communications software comes in a variety of media, depending upon the necessary distribution for the host being tied into the network. For most larger systems, it will be on a magnetic tape in a format suitable to the host operating system or one of its tape manipulation utilities. On smaller systems, the software may come on floppies or small tape cartridges. In any case, you will most likely need to specify the type of distribution that you would like from the vendor when you purchase the network.

Some media is configured on a node-by-node basis. This is done to simplify the installation process and to keep users (and companies) from copying the software on to new nodes that need to access the network. With the installation of a LAN, the network transfer of software is much more simplified than the transfer of software through media distribution such as floppies and tapes. This means that the temptation to "copy it over and install it" is greater in the networked environment and reduces the profitability of the company selling its networking products to customers, not to mention the legal issues involved. Be prepared to specify system configurations to the vendor, as it may require them for creation of distribution kits.

Most communications software is installed either in existing systems directories or in specific directories created by the installation process. Additionally, communications software will usually involve some sort of driver to talk to the hardware, a network kernel that handles all the networking functions, and user interfaces in the form of command parsers, utilities, or program libraries for programming purposes. The software may come pre-built (in executable form), object form and built on the system, or in source form for customization purposes. In all cases, the network software will require some host installation procedure that will be performed by the software installer (usually the system manager or the user of the network). Such procedures are in the form of installation programs, procedure files, batch files, or written commands that are typed in by the software installer in accordance with directions in an installation guide.

With most software installations comes an installation verification procedure (IVP) or test suite of programs or procedures to check out the software and insure that it has been installed properly and functions as expected. It is very useful to perform all test procedures to insure that the installation was successful and that the components do, in fact, function properly.

11. Configuration of the Network Database

Most communications architectures require that a database be kept on each node for a variety of purposes such as counters, event monitors, error logging, routing, and many other purposes. Some products configure the database themselves upon the initial activation of the network. Others have a program that asks simple questions and generates the database for the user. Still other products require a complete, manual effort on the part of the network administrator. In all cases, a database must be generated so that the network knows who is who, where the various nodes are, what the topology looks like, etc... A database must be configured for every node. This can be an important item to remember, as some networks will not allow the nodes to communicate with each other until the network databases have been properly set-up and configured.

12. Activation of the Network Software

The last step to activation of the network itself is the activation of the network software. Network software is usually activated as a background process, a batch process, or on-demand (as in the case on PC's). The software is usually activated by batch procedures or by specific network programs that are included in the distribution. Activation of a particular node may cause an "event" to occur on the network and all other nodes may respond. An event is, simply, an action on the network that can change the status or configuration of the network. A new node activating changes the configuration of the network, hence an event has happened.

13. Testing of Network Hardware/Software

Now that the software and hardware has been installed, all components of the LAN architecture should be tested. Most vendors will include programs for testing the various components and methods of access. Over and above those test procedures, it is necessary for the support group to sit down and get very familiar with the network components prior to allowing users to have access to the LAN. This step is very important to proper support and understanding of the LAN technology. As a rule, the following tests should be done:

o Test all file transfer capabilities with all supported file types (Most networks support sequential file access, but others support relative files and indexed files as well. Test them all).

o Test all file types with the various operating systems. Make sure that all possible combinations are tested.

o If the network supports it, try sending multiple files to a single node simultaneously to test network synchronization and access.

o If virtual terminal software is provided, try connecting to the various systems and exercise all aspects of the link software (screen editing, forms, graphics, etc...)

o Write some sample network programs to test the network application libraries as well as to verify the programmability of the network for future applications. Many times the library used to generate network utilities is not the same library as distributed to users for programming. Test it out!

o Put any network control utilities through the paces. Use them in a typical environment. Try to break the network. The users will.

o If any applications you are currently using claim to support the LAN you have selected, test them as well. Do it before the users have a chance to do it to preclude any embarassing questions or problems.

o Disconnect nodes and verify network stability. Take systems up and down in the middle of network sessions to check error control and recovery. If you can figure out a way to disrupt the network, try it. The vendor may claim that the damage you do is unsupported, but if you know the symptoms in a controlled situation, you can handle the problem when it arises on the live LAN.

Vigorously exercise all components and capabilities of the network BEFORE users get access to it. You will never get the chance to play with the network and test out the various components after that happens due to firefighting, question answering, and support duties.

14. Throughput Analysis

As part of any LAN installation, it is essential to know what the best case throughput will be, the average, and the worst. This is necessary in determining if the LAN is responding properly and data is moving at expected rates. Highly scientific tests are not too useful in throughput testing, as when the network degrades, there is no time for a highly scientific analysis procedure. The cry that will be heard is "Fix it!" Users do not care about the hows and whys. All they usually want is to get the functions completed that they want to do and not much else.

Throughput can be measured in a variety of ways. I usually write a small program that sends data across a network as fast as it can to a receiving task and time the results. I then keep the program on all nodes so that I can set up a test at any time I want. Other methods include utilizing batch files that show the time and size of a file before transfer and show the time after transfer with a display, if possible, of network counters before and after. So, throughput testing procedures can be complex or simple, but complex is usually not real. Simple is closer to everyday life in the LAN environment.

When testing throughput, take time to set up different test scenarios. Load up some systems and try to access them to see what happens (some networks bomb, some sit and wait, others timeout, etc.). Remember also that topology can be your enemy in a networked environment. If your LAN uses a common routing node for all traffic (like in a central star topology), that single node can degrade the entire network. So, in addition to testing for raw throughput, make sure you know what is affecting the LAN and where throughput bottlenecks may exist.

15. User Training

Users have to be trained. They don't think so, but they really need it.

Users typically fall into two categories: the "I'll figure it out myself" types and the "I'm afraid I'll break it" types. Kind of the yin and yang of users, if you want to look at it that way. The "I'll figure it out myself" types can be the hardest to deal with, as they feel that they have enough background with the systems that learning the network is not a big deal. They will also be the most difficult to deal with, as they will ask (nay, demand) answers to totally irrelevant questions to what they are trying to accomplish and will raise the roof when they are dismissed as trivial or unnecessary. Also, this type of user typically wants a copy of all the documentation as he/she is somewhat distrustful of the support group and feels better doing it themselves.

On the other end are those who feel a computer will break when they touch it and tend to have an inane fear of technology. These are most willing to have you help them along, but they must be weaned from protective support after a while or they will never get over their apprehension of the system or the LAN.

There are those users who fall somewhere in the middle, but, oddly enough, they are fairly rare. These are usually the less panicky, more stable types who take things in stride and provide stability for the environment.

To cover the training needs for most users, the best method is a tutorial approach (with exercises and self tests) that allows the user to read, try, review, and test him/herself on what was learned. Through this method, support group productivity remains high while the learning curve is being built by the user base. In addition to the tutorial training, periodic classroom training should be done to reinforce the tutorial exercises as well as to expand into areas not covered by the tutorial training method. Through a combination of these two methods, users can become proficient in LAN usage in a short amount of time and keep the support staff productive in the process.

16. Turnover for Use

By now, the users have been trained, the support staff trained, applications tested, etc., etc., etc... It would logically follow to declare the LAN usable and available, right? Nope, not yet. Before the LAN can be turned over, the following needs to be in place:

o Problem support mechanism. When it breaks or questions arise, who solves the problems?
o Security administration policies need to be updated for the networked environment. Because LANs, by nature, are somewhat non-secure, the entire network could potentially be compromised through the actions of a single user on a particular node. If a user with system access privileges were to attack, vigorously, any network, it would be a matter of time before the entire network and any systems attached to it would be penetrated. **A network is only as secure as its least secure node.**
o Support and maintenance contracts with the vendor need to be finalized and known to the support group. Finding out where to get help before it is needed is always preferable to getting a runaround when help is critical.
o User guides and manuals need to be produced, copied, and distributed for LAN users. These documents are dissimilar to the tutorials in that they provide ready-reference capabilities to LAN users.
o Management and control procedures need to be established to allow for how the network will be controlled, how upgrades will be done, backups and restores, and many other management-related tasks.
o Disaster recovery plans need to be modified to reflect the needs and usage of the network in a recovery operation following a disaster.
o Other related items...

From this list, it is easy to see that LANs involve much more than the technology installation and use, but also the management and support of the technology implemented.

Chapter Summary

Installing an Ethernet requires that all the above issues be considered and planned for a successful installation. Network installations are very different from software installations and are more similar to an actual systems installation. Properly planned and executed, a network installation can be very successful and provide a productive, maintainable environment.

Chapter Nine

Ethernet Installation
Hints and Kinks

Why shouldn't truth be stranger than fiction. Fiction, after all, has to make sense.

Mark Twain

Introduction

In this chapter, we will look at various methods and techniques to install Ethernets with emphasis on installation in the DEC environment.

You may find upon reading this chapter that there is some information that is duplicated from previous chapters. This was done intentionally to re-emphasize the importance as well as to keep from having to refer back to previous pages and chapters. I find this to be very annoying when I am trying to figure out what is going on, so I have included the pertinent information again where reasonable.

The Cable

Basically, there are three types of Ethernet cable (or Etherhose as many networking types affectionately refer to the cable): baseband coax, broadband coax, and thinwire (RG58) coax. Most sites utilizing the standard DEC type of Ethernet will be utilizing the broadband coax which is also referred to as Beldon 9880 (Beldon's cable type), AWM E60862 Style 1478, or DEC part number 17-00451-01 (they also call it BNE2x-xx). Other sites utilizing broadband technology may use RG6 or RG11 to RG59 broadband coax with RF MODEMs to allow the systems to communicate with the broadband network. Thinwire users will find the familiar RG58 thin coaxial cable almost anywhere (including places like Radio Shack and on the back of your television if you have cable television). Be careful that you do not get RG58 confused with RG59. Ethernet cable is terminated for 50 ohms, which is great for RG58. RG59, while similar in appearance, is 75 ohms and, therefore, incompatible. All three types of cable plants allow the functionality of Ethernet and, with the appropriate interconnection equipment, can be connected together. Which cable plant is selected depends upon the networking need. Broadband is typically seen where the need is to provide data networking, video, voice (PBX-PBX), and extended distance networking. Baseband, the easiest to implement and much less expensive than broadband, is usually seen where speed is an issue or flexibility of installation is necessary. Thinwire networks typically work in a baseband manner, but are used in office environments where a flexible cable plant is necessary due to frequent office layout changes and there are a substantial number of connection points. In all cases, however, there are some standard "do's" that should always be included in the design and installation.

Growth Planning

First off, always plan for about a 100% growth in network connections in the first year. I've seen, many times, the initial plan for the network expand, exponentially, the first year. This is usually due to lack of management recognition of the capabilities of a local area network (LAN) and the effort by management to get maximum utilization of resources after initial installation. A bank customer of mine once asked for an Ethernet for 10 PC's so that they could communicate to a previously installed thick-wire baseband Ethernet. I complied with the request and designed a network which they thought would accommodate 10 nodes. In reality, I designed it for 100 nodes knowing full well that banks are rife with politics and other VP's would see the PC's and want the same capability. As things turned out, I was correct. 10 months later, the network consisted not of 10 PC's but of 82 PC's with additional VAXes to handle the additional loading. What frequently starts off as a small network grows large very quickly. This is not an isolated incidence; it happens quite frequently to many companies. Lesson to learn: think ahead.

Pre-installation inspection.

When cable installation time rolls around, always pre-inspect the areas where the cable is to be installed to preclude any surprises. It's very frustrating to have to run the Ethernet to places where no wire has gone before. Check where the cable is supposed to go carefully and insure that there is proper cable space, access ways, and routing information (where the cable will go and how it will be laid).

Cable testing.

Always, always, always check the cable out while it is still on the reel. After the cable is installed in the wireways is the wrong time to find out that it was flawed to begin with. Most cable vendors have a device called a time domain reflectometer (TDR) that can be connected to the cable while on the reel. One end of the cable is terminated properly and the TDR hooked up to the other end and an electrical signal is sent down the wire. If the results show that the cable is infinitely long, the cable is solid and good. If the TDR reports that the cable is, say, 10 meters long, there is a disruption of some sort at that point and it should be examined and repaired or replaced. It also helps to do this electronic examination in front of cable installation teams to show them that the cable is good and it had better be that way after it is pulled!

Cable marking

As the cable is being installed (cable people call this pulling cable), use some white athletic tape and mark the cable every five meters, writing the mark on the tape on the cable. Following this, mark a building map with the cable marking locations for later reference. Finally, use some small, colored labels (Avery has an entire rainbow of colors) and write the cable marker number on them. Place the labels either on the baseboard of the walls under which the cable is laid or on the ceiling in some inconspicuous spot if run through the ceiling. Later, when the cable fails (it WILL - someday), a TDR session will find the elusive break or short, and tracing the exact location on the cable will be greatly simplified.

Cable segmentation

Everyone I know has an opinion on this. So, to preclude too much controversy, I am going to suggest only one item for now. If your Ethernet cable is fairly long (over 200 meters) or has a high number of nodes on it (over 30), put a barrel connector in the cable at either 23.4 meters, 70.2 meters, or 117 meter segments (in actuality, if the cable is to be segmented with barrel connectors at all, they should be segmented into pieces of the aforeprescribed lengths). Yes, Virginia, it's one more thing to cause a failure, but how often do barrel connectors fail? Pretty rarely, in my experience. Why do it? Well, we know that the network will fail at some time. By placing the connector in the middle, the cable can be disconnected in the middle (separating it into two segments) and the two segments terminated with 50 ohm terminators. The effect: one half of the cable is going to come up and one half will not. This allows the network manager to concentrate efforts on the side that has failed and reduces the search time for the fault. For those who are concerned about potential EMI or RFI problems, you need not. A friend at DEC once told me the story of how they tested the Ethernet cable for interference while the technology was under development at DEC. It seems that there were some skeptics on the shielding capabilities of the cable, so they placed a live segment of the cable under a powerful FM radio tower. Following this, a test was conducted with various connectors, transceivers, and other RF-admitting devices to see what would happen with collisions and other problems (such as noise). In the test, very few collisions were noted, even under such adverse conditions. Final result? Specification-compliant thick-wire Ethercable is very well insulated and durable. Adding an additional barrel connector should not increase the potential for problems and will help isolate problems when they occur.

Cable types.

Basically, there are two types of cable: PVC (which is usually yellow in color) and Teflon (usually orange). The general rule is to use Teflon anywhere the cable will run that allows recirculation of air to humans, but check your local fire and city codes for clarification. Sure, PVC is cheaper, but consider this: do you want to be in the same area as

PVC cable if it is burning? Not me. PVC can give off cyanide gas when burning, which can tend to ruin your whole day in a big hurry! Yes, I know that 99% of the silly grey twisted pair cables in ceilings are PVC, so who cares? Fire codes often state that previous to the regulation cable plants are exempt, but new cables must comply with the fire codes; CHECK! Teflon, however, has problems as well. Teflon, like most glass products, is not a true solid material. As a result, constriction of Teflon Ethercable will cause a condition called "cold flow" and cause the Teflon to migrate in a cable. What this translates to is that bends in Teflon cable that are tighter than a 9" bend radius tend to accelerate this condition and may, over a period of time, cause a short in the cable (which, of course, kills the network). For those of you who are concerned about this, it's not that serious, but something to be avoided. Should you find that such a condition has occurred, it's a simple matter to remove the offending piece of cable and splice in a new section. By the way, DEC and Beldon don't seem to concerned about the bend radius. They ship Ethernet cable on 4" reels.

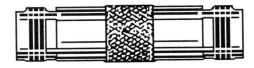

A Barrel Connector

Tapping thickwire

Thickwire Ethernets (the most common - for now) are non-intrusively tapped. This means that, supposedly, a connection being added to the cable will not disturb the network activity in progress. In truth, this is usually the case unless the installer goofs up and causes a short on the cable or the installed transceiver (or other component) decides to cause major problems on the cable. The procedure is fairly simple:

1. Find a black marker ring on the cable. They are 2.5 meters apart.

2. Secure the cable with a cable guide. In the case of the DEC H4000A, there is a bracket with a set of plastic drill guides that are clamped on the cable. If you are using an H4000B (which uses the popular AMP upper assembly that is used by many vendors), there is a slide mount assembly that slides over the cable and is secured to the cable with a screw. In both cases, the drill guide on the H4000A and the tap guide hole on the H4000B should appear directly over a black ring in the cable.

3. Once the guide is positioned, the tap is made. Taps should always be made on the black ring to insure that interference on the cable is kept to a minimum and for other RF reasons that would take too long to explain in this article. A hole is drilled in the cable to remove the outer coating and braid shielding to allow the transceiver to be connected to the cable. The hole is necessary as the transceiver has a metal spine that goes through the hole that is created and connects to the center conductor of the cable, taking care not to also contact the outer layer of shielding (this would cause a short and the network will fail). On H4000A's the hole is made with a battery-powered drill; on H4000B's the hole is made with a small orange handtool. In the case of the H4000A, it is **EXTREMELY IMPORTANT** that the drill be properly grounded, hence the usage of a battery powered drill. If an AC drill is used and not properly grounded, a ground loop can occur on the cable and the result may be disastrous: transceivers up and down the cable may be burnt out by the resultant loop. To compound the problem, the H4000A requires that two holes be punched in the cable at opposite sides to each other. One hole is not difficult to punch, but the secondary hole may be quite miserable. On installed cables, and long cables, the cable will frequently rotate even though the cable guide may seem firmly in place. As a result, it can be quite tedious to get correctly punched holes in the cable. If you have an H4000A (they are large, black, and the entire case is made of plastic), get someone to help keep the cable in place during a tap session - it reduces the aggravation factor substantially. When the holes have been drilled, remove the required Digital-spec drill bit and manually ream out the hole a little with the drill bit or with a dentist's pick to insure that all braid has been removed and to remove the various stray bits of insulation and trash that accumulate. On the H4000B, tapping is greatly simplified (thank you, Uncle Digital) by the use of the handtool and the cable guide that is actually the upper assembly of the transceiver. In both cases, remove any accumulated items with a suitable tool; do not blow into the hole as all you will do is seat the offending remains of braid and insulation or, possibly, cause a moisture accumulation (yes, I know that sounds dumb but it can happen).

4. Attach the transceiver. The H4000A is a little tricky to connect as the top and bottom holes in the cable both receive a spine. It is, therefore, very important that the cable not twist while attaching the transceiver. To assist in this, there are two small brads that fit into two holes on either side of the spine location in the bottom section of the transceiver in the cable receiver trough. The brads have a small, pliable "jaw" on the top of the brad with a long wire end that slides into the transceiver cable trough holes. The jaw of each brad grips the cable to help hold it into place during the cable installation and after the transceiver has been tightened on the cable. In the case of the H4000A, four hands are useful in the insertion of the cable in the cable trough to keep it from twisting as well as to insure that the spines will align properly during the installation of the upper assembly of the transceiver. One set of hands should grip the cable and hold it in place while the other set places the upper slide on the transceiver and tightens it down with the DEC-supplied hex wrench that is needed to tighten down the center spine and upper receiver. Tighten each wrench position a little at a time to insure that the entire upper assembly glides down evenly and presses firmly on the cable. When it is completely tightened down, the transceiver is locked in. In the case of the H4000B, the upper receiver of the transceiver is also the cable guide, so once the cable guide has been locked into position, the hole that is made by the installer simply fits over the protruding spine on the lower receiver of the H4000B. The unit is locked down and the tap is complete. The H4000B has brads, like the H4000A, but these are seen when the cable is being initially fitted into the guide. In both cases, the brads' jaws will squeeze shut on the cable insulation as the transceiver is tightened on to the cable (this is why most Etherpeople call the brads "vampire clamps"). With either type of H4000 comes a box of replacement brads in the case that a transceiver is removed and will be used elsewhere.

It is important to point out a couple of things when drilling holes in Ethercable. First, if you mess up (and you will mess up at some time or another), simply move a few inches either one way or another and drill again. It will not cause radical breakdown of cable integrity to do so. Second, if you leave a hole in the cable without a transceiver in it, put a wrap of tape around the hole to keep trash from getting in it. If you feel the urge for something more substantial, try a dab of silicone sealer. Do NOT fill the hole with anything conductive, such as solder or the like - it will cause a cable short and the network will fail.

5. Cable slides. In the case of 802.3-compliant components, someone came up with a "new way" of connecting D-connectors (they're called that because, if viewed straight on, they look like the letter D) to components utilizing protruding studs that slide into notches in a connector. The studs are then secured to the connector by a slide mechanism that slides over the studs and corresponding notched openings, holding the connectors together. In theory, it's a great idea. Connect D-connectors without screws or tools. In application, however, the connectors used in Ethernet are too heavy for such an arrangement and cause serious problems with the slide mechanism (it bends and loosens or, in some situations, breaks off). To keep this from happening, utilize plastic tie-downs to secure the transceiver cable to the Ethernet cable. This is easily done by taking a tie down and placing is around the Ethernet cable and the transceiver cable about 3-4" from the transceiver end and tightening up the tie down. Tie downs are cheap (I think that a bag of 1000 are going for about $6.00) and easy to install. The only drawback is that they are, by nature, non-reusable, but you normally will not be moving transceivers around on a regular basis anyway. In all cases, use plenty of strain relief on connectors and cables to keep the connectors from separating from each other and to keep things from being jostled loose if the cables are moved or pulled upon.

6. Always label all transceiver cables and transceivers so that you know what systems they connect to the Ethernet. There is nothing more time consuming than trying to figure out who is connected to what. Label first and enjoy later.

7. If you are using transceivers from a vendor other than the one who supplied your Ethernet controller, make sure that you understand that, in accordance with spec, you are not a compliant installation. The Ethernet specifications are quite clear: the same vendor must supply the controller and transceiver for the connection to be within the specification. In many cases, other manufacturer's transceivers work well with many vendor's Ethernet controllers, but the mixed-vendor combination is sure to cause finger pointing when problems arise in addition to violating the specification.

Transceiver installation is not difficult if approached systematically. Make sure that you have all the proper components before you begin the tap operation. Remember that not all new equipment arrives in a functional state, so don't be too surprised if a transceiver acts up or does not work.

Controllers and Software Drivers

A great many communications companies offer Ethernet controllers. In the DEC case, there are QBUS and UNIBUS controllers for PDP-11 and MicroVAX systems available from many vendors. Other companies offer Ethernet controllers for VME, NuBus, Micro channel, A100, and many other popular bus structures. In all cases, it is important to point out that some controllers, such as DEC controllers, with the exception of PC Ethernet controllers, are REQUIRED for proper DECnet software operation. While it is quite true that you could plug in an Excelan Ethernet controller and utilize Ethernet, Digital's DECnet product will not work with it. DECnet requires that the host system load software components into the controller and that the controller know what to do with the loaded software. In DEC's case, only DEC controllers know what to do with DEC-loaded software (DECnet) and how to respond to DECnet requests. To date, I have not found a compatible 3rd-party controller that will work with DECnet at this time. That does not mean that they do not exist, only I have not found one that is 100% compatible. Ironically, the XXDRIVER.EXE, seen in the DECnet microfiche, was originally used to develop DECnet before the DEUNA was available. It used a 3rd-party Ethernet controller for testing and development purposes and was never supported outside DEC's engineering organization. So, it can be done, but such support is unlikely from DEC who wants to keep control of the market.

DEC's Ethernet controllers allow the capability of connecting to IEEE 802.3 Ethernets as well as Xerox/Intel/DEC V2.0 Ethernets. Also, most controllers allow the ability to connect multiple protocols, simultaneously, through the controller and driver. In the case of the Ethernet driver in VMS operating system, this is achieved through the rather clever use of two software drivers, one that talks to the controller directly (ESDRIVER.EXE) and one (a pseudo driver) that talks to the driver that talks to the controller (XEDRIVER.EXE for UNIBUS systems, XQDRIVER.EXE for QBUS, ETDRIVER.EXE for BI, and ESDRIVER.EXE for MicroVAX 2000 systems). The pseudo driver allows the creation of separate Unit Control Blocks (UCBs) for each new protocol so that each new protocol "looks" like a new device to VMS. The effect is easy to see. Start up DECnet and then execute the DCL command SHOW DEVICE and you will find more than one device for the first Ethernet controller. The first device (XEA0: on UNIBUS systems) is the actual controller. Subsequent devices (such as XEA6:, XEA7:, etc...) are actually virtual devices created by the protocol declarations when the protocol is declared by a connecting program. The net effect is that the same controller is capable of supporting more than one protocol at a time. This means that it is quite possible to run DECnet (it actually uses more than one protocol), TCP/IP, XNS, LAT, and who knows what other protocol.

Protocols may be single user or sharable, depending on how they are set up by the calling program. So, before you get controller happy and feel that you need different Ethernet controllers for different protocols, think again and consider a software alternative. Be careful, however, of some vendor's software solutions. Some are not coded very well and use up a disproportionate amount of system resources to provide connectivity services.

By the way, while I'm harping on controllers, beware of "new technology" controllers. That usually means new firmware and new "undocumented features" (bugs). Many customers have been bitten by the new technologies that appear from time to time. If your network applications are critical, make sure that you get a chance to test the controller out before committing a critical workload to it. You may be in for a rough ride.

On the down side, many 3rd party controllers support many popular protocols in the controller, effectively offloading the host system. This can be very useful in helping your system along when managing multiple protocols on the Ethernet and may be a good incentive to consider dual controllers on a particular system. When installing dual controllers, make sure that you consider bus contention, power consumption, etc., before you purchase the controller, as the multi-controller environment requires some planning. Don't worry about Ethernet addressing, however. All Ethernet cards have one unique address that is inserted, usually in ROM, by the manufacturer. In the case of DEC cards utilizing Ethernet and DECnet there are two addresses involved: the ROM (hardware) address and a virtual address (in controller RAM) that DECnet places in the controller. This second address is based upon DECnet node number plus a specified adder that allows DECnet to know that it is talking, in fact, to a DECnet node as well as for other DEC uses. If you use an Ethernet analyzer, such as the Lanalyzer, and try to monitor the hardware address of a particular controller for DECnet traffic, you will be sadly disappointed. Try, instead, monitoring the DECnet virtual address and you will have success. By the way, the reason for this anomaly in the sea of Etherstandards is because Ethernet uses a 48-bit node address and DECnet only supports, at this time, 16-bit node addresses. Through DEC software trickery (involving the virtual address), DEC is able to fake out DECnet and allow 16-bit addresses where 48-bit addresses normally roam. A constant 32-bit number (AA-00-04-00) from DEC's assigned address range is used as a base and the 16-bit node address for a particular node is appended to it. For instance, if the node were a DECnet router and had an address of 1.182, the resultant "virtual" Ethernet address that would be loaded into the controller would be AA-00-04-00-B6-04.

Chapter Summary

Installation of Ethernet is not difficult if approached systematically. Certain vendors require certain types of "tricks" to get the network connected up properly to the systems involved. No installation is inordinately difficult, but some are trickier than others.

When considering installation of components on Ethernet-connected machines, carefully consider these notes and insight to make your implementation as trouble-free and easy as possible.

Chapter Ten

Troubleshooting Ethernets

Why would I want to change my mind? Is there something wrong with the one I have?

Mr. Spock (Star Trek IV)

Introduction

Ethernets break. Most things do from time to time. Problem is that most things that break rarely come with an instruction guide as to what to do when they do break. In this chapter we will explore the various general techniques available to troubleshoot failed Ethernets.

It is important to point out that with the variety of Ethernets and variety of software implementations that it is quite impossible to document all the possible ways that an Ethernet failure may be isolated. Always consult your specific Ethernet documentation on fault detection and isolation that is provided by the vendor of the Ethernet plant that is being used.

As broadband technologies are more difficult to troubleshoot and require a greater level of understanding in the specific implementation involved, this chapter is dedicated to baseband Ethernet fault isolation. If you have a broadband network, you will require additional education on the selected vendor's technology as broadband networks function somewhat differently than baseband Ethernet and each vendor has slightly different mechanism for broadband implementation. You may still find, however, that some of the described techniques will be useful in troubleshooting certain classes of broadband Ethernet problems.

An important, but omitted, topic is that of software problem isolation. As there are many different types of software packages available for the Ethernet environment and just as many types of tools and software diagnostic and error detection mechanisms, a useful discussion is practically impossible and is also out of the scope of this book. You are strongly encouraged to understand, fully, how your particular software technology links up to Ethernet and how to troubleshoot the software when it fails. And it will. Count on it.

General Troubleshooting Guidelines

As a general rule, there are certain guidelines to follow when troubleshooting networks and these apply rigorously to the Ethernet environment:

a) **Always try to deal with the obvious items first.** Newly installed components are usually a good place to start. Failing that, examine obvious sources of information such as network software event logs, error counters, or any other such indicator that may point to an obvious location where the error occurs.

b) **Set up and use a checklist of what was done and in what order.** Some network testing and diagnostics require that certain actions take place in a certain sequence to insure that a particular component is properly isolated. By keeping to a checklist, network fault finding activity can be documented and not replicated over and over again in futility.

c) **Keep detailed logs of previous network faults and resolutions involved.** Such logs are frequently very handy when trying to find faults or solutions to faults. On larger networks, faults may occur regularly and require that the same fixes be used periodically in different parts of the network. Utilizing a log helps the network manager remember what the fault was, how it was isolated, and how it was fixed. There is no substitute for good documentation of isolated and repaired faults.

d) **Always try to isolate whether the problem is with a particular node or a specific group of nodes.** Through this type of isolation, common elements may be found and corrected in a hurry. Haphazard searches do not help find the fault unless it is by accident. Knowing if the fault is only with a particular node helps simplify the problem of resolution to a great degree.

e) **Learn to use vendor-specified or supplied software and hardware tools BEFORE the network breaks.** The network IS going to break; you may as well accept that as an axiom. Therefore, learning to use the diagnostic tools after the failure has occurred is a little late. Get comfortable with the tools at your disposal and learn to read the results when the network is functioning properly and when it is not.

f) **Usage of network monitoring tools may be useful in detecting a network fault, but not always.** Never rely entirely upon a particular tool or set of tools to provide an absolute answer. Software versions change, microcode versions change, ECOs are applied to hardware. Because of this, diagnostics may break or, worse, lie. Network monitor tools are also statistical sampling tools to a great extent and may not provide a great deal of information that is useful in making real-time repair decisions. Evaluate the usefulness of tools carefully lest the tools be improperly relied upon for critical information that they cannot and will not provide when trying to isolate a fault.

In all situations, utilization of a cool head and common sense is very useful in isolating network failures. Diagnosing a failure can be a very stressful time and snap decisions are easy to make but can end up taking more time than a methodical approach will take. Use your time wisely, evaluate, carefully, the situation, and select your starting point accordingly.

Above all, use common sense.

Cable Failures

The most common failure on an Ethernet is the failure of the Ethernet cable itself. This is usually caused by "human" interference: someone kicking a transceiver, pulling a thinwire cable too far from the back of a PC, dropping a terminator (there's a ceramic resistor in there, you know), a bad tap that causes a short in the cable, or other such maloccurence.

Fixing cable problems is not a difficult thing to do. Bad taps are easily remedied by removing the bad tap. Most of the time the network will reactivate properly. Broken cables can be re-connected by installing a barrel connector where the break occurred. Dislocated transceivers can easily be either re-aligned or re-installed a few inches from the original tap. In most cases, fixing the cable is not a big issue and easily executed.

Finding the break or short in the cable is another story. On a 400-meter Ethernet with 50 taps, how can you find the offending tap? Or, better yet, where is the break in the cable? Where do you even start to look?

The foremost ally in the fight to find the fault is proper cable marking and a time domain reflectometer. Cable marking, as previously described, is not difficult but must be done at the time the cable is installed. Cable is marked at regular intervals while the cable is being pulled. Additionally, the cable is also color coded in those installations where multiple Ethernet cables may appear in common wire trays or run areas. Marking the cables is essential when trying to locate cable faults. By using a time domain reflectometer (TDR), a network manager can connect the TDR to the end of the Ethernet cable and use the TDR to locate the break or short. How is this done? Quite simple, actually. The TDR sends a signal down the cable and then waits for a reflection of the signal. When the reflected signal is received, the TDR evaluates the amount of time that was required to receive the reflection and, from that difference, can calculate the distance from the TDR to the location on the cable where the signal was reflected. If the cable is deemed to be "infinitely" long, it is unbroken and in a functional condition. If the cable is, say, 50 meters long according to the TDR, the Ethernet most likely has a short or a break at the distance from the TDR specified by the TDR. A TDR is a very valuable tool for locating, exactly, where a break or short occurs on a cable.

One issue to be considered with a TDR is the case of a failed terminator. Terminators must be installed on both ends of an Ethernet cable when the cable is installed and functioning. To attach a TDR, one end of the cable must have its terminator removed so that the TDR may be attached to the network. This, obviously, causes a short on the network and the network will fail. If the network cable shows being infinitely long, it is possible that the terminator that was removed may be bad. To test the terminator, simply use an ohmmeter and place one probe on the center of the terminator and ground the other probe to the outside casing of the terminator. If the terminator does not register between 48 and 52 ohms, the terminator is bad and must be replaced. Replacement is very simple: screw in a new terminator to the N connector on the end of the cable. Always check the terminators if the cable disruption is not obvious. The test is simple and quick.

If the Ethernet being used is of the thinwire, thickwire broadband, twisted pair, or fiber optic variety, many TDRs have different adapters for usage with the various medium types. In the case of fiber, however, a specialized TDR may be required for particular types of fiber. OTDRs or FOTDRs come in various types depending upon fiber type (graded index, stepped index, single mode, or multimode) and light source used to test out the cable.

Finding the break in an Ethernet cable is easily done if the cable is tested methodically. If a TDR is not available, using an ohmmeter can help isolate if the cable is properly terminated. Again, measure the cable in the manner described for the terminator (it should also measure between 48 and 52 ohms). While an ohmmeter cannot tell where a break has occurred, it can help to determine the cable is properly balanced.

In situations where a TDR is not available, finding the break in the cable can be difficult at best. Try the following steps when isolating cable faults:

1. Check out recently installed transceivers or connectors to insure that they are properly installed and functional. Some transceivers may cause a static charge to be built up over a period of time that can cause a short. Movement of improperly aligned transceivers may cause the same. In all cases, newly installed components are a good place to start checking to see if the fault has occurred.

2. Installation of barrel connectors at 23.4, 70.2, or 117 meter increments will allow the cable to be isolated in case of failure. The reason for the specified lengths is to keep noise and harmonic distortion to a minimum while still allowing segmentation of the network. At the barrel connectors, simply remove the "barrel" from the N connectors on each side and install 50 ohm terminators in each N connector. This will cause the network to be divided into segments that will be terminated properly. As a result, the network segments with no faults will activate properly and the failing segment will not activate. This allows concerted effort to be applied where the break or short is projected to be and not in areas where the problem does not exist.

3. Occasionally, certain makes of transceiver will cause network cable failures when the transceiver fails in a certain way. In those cases, the transceiver may need to be powered down before the fault will clear. Powering down transceivers is a tedious job that requires the transceiver cable from the transceiver to the controller on the system to be either disconnected from the transceiver or from the system side. Pin 13 on the transceiver cable provides positive voltage to the transceiver from the controller. The only way to turn the power off is to either install a switch in the transceiver cable pin 13 or to disconnect the controller from the transceiver. In either case, once the transceiver is disconnected from power, it is rendered useless, and if an electrical fault in the transceiver is causing the problem, the problem should clear.

In unusual situations, the transceiver may cause its internal circuitry to become fused due to a power surge or other such electrical fault. If this should happen, powering down the transceiver may not solve the problem. This means that the individual transceivers on a failed segment may need to be individually removed from the segment until the offending transceiver is found and replaced.

Most of the time, the prescribed methods of cable fault isolation will allow the network manager to locate and correct the cable fault. In all situations, however, a methodical search must be done to insure that nothing obvious is overlooked or necessary steps in isolation are avoided.

Transceiver Failure

Transceiver failure is usually rare, but it does occur. In some cases, only the node connected to a particular transceiver may fail, making the isolation of the failing component somewhat easier. In more severe cases, the transceiver may "babble" or place sporadic noise on the cable. Collisions occur, but cannot be isolated to any particular reason. If a network has been functioning well and all of a sudden the collision rate increases for no explainable reason, a transceiver may be running amok.

Most transceivers have error-detection circuitry and report errors back to the controller. Some models of transceivers do not and can cause problems and not report them. Consult your vendor documentation carefully and learn about your selected transceiver's weaknesses and strengths.

Some transceivers from some vendors have LEDs on them to indicate errors or conditions that are not normal. Other types have on-board diagnostics that can be run through a system software command or through DIP switch settings in the transceiver. In all cases, failed transceivers may be isolated by observing visual signals, running diagnostics, or simply disconnecting the transceiver from the host system (cutting its power).

Cases where a transceiver is not showing any outward cause of failure and still the network is having troubles may indicate a periodic transceiver failure. Transceivers may fail, off and on, for a variety of reasons such as weak power supplies, transceiver cables that are too long, and other problems. In those cases where such failures occur, individualized removal from the network may be necessary to isolate the offending transceiver. Start by electrically isolating the transceiver (power it off) and then, if that fails, start looking into a short situation or possibly a loose connection or tap.

Another test is a loopback test through to the end of the transceiver cable. A 15-pin D connector is attached to the location where the transceiver would normally connect at the end of the cable. Once connected, the host system (with the communications software activated) would typically "see" itself due to the signal reflections coming through the loopback connector. If a host "sees" itself, then the system connection is good to at least the end of the cable where the cable connects to the transceiver. If a system does not see itself, there is something else wrong (such as the transceiver cable or possibly the controller).

In addition to the loopback plug, there are loopback transceivers as well. These perform the same basic function as the loopback connector except they also may allow further testing of the controller due to special features that may be included in the transceiver unit.

In all cases, a failed transceiver is one of the hardest things to identify if the transceiver has not failed totally and permanently. Be prepared for some investigative work to isolate the faulty transceiver. Keep activity and error logs and eventually the guilty component will confess.

Controller Failures

Controllers can be one of the easier components to isolate in the case of a failure. Most of the time, vendors install self-test diagnostics on-board the controller that allows it to check itself out upon power-up or initialization sequences. Many software packages supply a network control program that will allow the network manager to force the controller into a self-diagnostic mode or reset mode. Learn to use the tools to allow such action to take place.

Sometimes controllers can cause a failure because it gets "confused." Reinitialization of the controller may cause it to get itself straightened out and functioning correctly. A side effect, however, is the fact that if the controller is getting confused on a regular basis, there is something more serious afoot. Reinitialization of the controller will typically clear out any current settings that may point to a particular failure, so do not jump up and cause the controller to reinitialize every time an error is suspected. Use diagnostic tools to examine the failed components register values and other such telltale mechanisms to find and correct a recurring or unique problem.

Many Ethernet controllers are too smart for their own good. Since vendors have discovered the benefits of using "smart" Ethernet controllers, some controllers now have more operating system code and processor horsepower than the system to which they are attached. The end result is that bugs and other undesirable features may creep in to the architecture and materialize at inopportune times. Close monitoring of the network events and errors will help isolate such occurrences.

Controllers usually provide a condition that is available called controller loopback. What happens is that the host system networking software forces the controller to echo back, exactly, any series of data that is sent. The host then compares what was sent to what was echoed back to see if there is a difference. If no difference, the controller is echoing back the information correctly and another problem may be causing the fault. If, however, the controller improperly echoes the originally sent information, it is a safe bet that the controller is not functioning properly and should be replaced.

As mentioned previously, the controllers built by many vendors are very sophisticated. As such, it is important to understand that controllers, like operating systems, periodically require upgrades and enhancements to internal microcode or ROM stored software. Controllers that have functioned reliably may cease to function properly, especially after a preventative maintenance cycle that included the installation of various ECO or FCO modifications to the controller or its firmware/ROM code.

Occasionally, a controller may look like it has problems when, in reality, it may have been initialized improperly by host software. Check host software to insure that it is setting proper controller values and intializing controller settings in a manner conducsive to good interplay between the host software and the software in the controller.

There are many things that can go wrong in a controller. By learning how to run the diagnostics and also how to re-initialize the controller, many problems can be quickly isolated or rectified. In those situations where the problem persists and the controller has been isolated as the culprit, it may be a flaw in the software in the controller or other such related item. This, obviously, requires a modification be made by the vendor and that can take time. Also, many vendors do not make snap code modifications to controllers without carefully examining the ramifications to other customers. Do not expect a rapid fix if the problem turns out to be a real bug in the controller firmware or ROM code.

Chapter Summary

Troubleshooting Ethernet is not difficult if approached systematically and with care. There are quite a few things that can fail - some at the same time. In all cases, failure rectification is usually easy. Fault isolation is the hard part.

Different types of techniques exist for correction of each type of Ethernet component failure. Obviously not all have been included, but enough have been to get the idea of what has to be done to find a fault. Consult vendor documentation for a proper discussion of what to do in case of a fault and how to isolate faults when they occur.

They will.

Chapter Eleven

Network Training

If a little knowledge is dangerous, where is a man [or woman] who has so much as to be out of danger?

Thomas Henry Huxley

Introduction

How many times have you received educational junk mail in your office in-basket? If you are like me, it is a pretty regular occurrence. As a matter of fact, I tend to believe that educational courseware promotional brochures account for over half the use of paper in the world today, but that is another story for another time. Out of those brochures, more and more companies are pushing network and network-related courses as part of their offerings (I know this because I see the same companies sending me networking brochures with the same instructors on them as the courses on introductory systems courses). Even the big boys, such as Digital, are spending more money and time getting their network course curricula developed to help meet the needs of the "exploding network marketplace."

I'm all for professionally made and delivered courses. As a matter of fact, I've developed quite a few myself and I have also delivered, literally, hundreds of seminars on a variety of subjects (particularly networks). I have noticed, however, that there are some areas that many folks never address when considering network education that are critical to understanding what is being received for the money spent. Like any good consumer, we all try to get the best value for the money spent. In these days of tight travel and educational budgets, it is even more critical that training we receive is what we need and of a quality that is useful to us when we return to the job. Therefore, in this article we shall explore network training: how it "happens," what to look for, who needs it, and how much does it cost.

Course Development

One of the first things to remember in any course that you may attend is the problem of course development. Have you ever seriously thought about the work and effort that goes into development of a course or, more importantly, what caused the course to be developed to start with? Well, it starts, usually, with market research. An enterprising company or individual identifies a need for network education, identifies a target marketplace, figures out how much money can be made, and presents his or her case to company management. If the marketing metrics are good, the company will typically identify course development resources, identify course developers, course instructors, set up a development schedule, and set up a course pilot delivery schedule to test the new course on potential consumers. When the course is developed and tested (the pilot courses), final modifications and enhancements are made, final handouts and labs produced, copies are made of all materials, and courses are scheduled for delivery to consumers. Obviously this is an abbreviated list of actions that take place, but it is easy to get the picture that course development, professionally done, takes time and effort and a great deal of resources.

Probably the toughest part of the course development cycle is finding a competent courseware developer for the network subject that has been identified. While it is true that there are a great many individuals who are competent network professionals, the real problem with network training is the issue of how to impart a networking professional's knowledge and experience into a new consumer in a reasonable and expedient fashion. Development of a course is not like delivering, or instructing, a course. The developer has to be acutely aware of how to present concepts, facts, and issues in a manner that both the instructor can present to the students and also so the students can understand the material from the instructor as it is presented. Therefore, a course developer has to have a unique set of qualifications if a course is to be successful. He has to be very knowledgeable (or develop the knowledge, but that takes more time) in the subject presented, know how to write for the consumer, understand the problems and concepts of educating students and instructors, plan lesson time according to content and what can be reasonably learned in the planned time frame, and, most importantly, be able to impart knowledge and experience to the student in a manner in which the student can use the knowledge gained when he/she returns to the job.

Now for reality. In many larger companies, the previously described methods of course development is the standard methodology used. Many times, however, companies interested in the "quick kill" or the ones that jump on the network bandwagon do not follow good, standardized course development procedures. The results can be catastrophic for everyone involved. I've attended courses where the instructors did not know how to teach their subject or did not have any idea as to what they were teaching, either because the course was not developed properly or the instructor was not familiar with the subject being presented. One time, years ago, I attended a seminar on network queueing theory that got me so confused that it took me four months to get myself straightened out and then I found out what I had "learned" was WRONG!! Boy, was I hacked! I spent a good deal of time trying to explain what I learned to my co-workers, some of which did not understand what I was relaying (thank goodness that was my first sign that something was amiss) to them as a result of the course. Others knew enough about the subject to let me know that something was not right about what I had been told. I then went in a search for truth and found that I had been misled. It proved to be very embarrassing for me, for my co-workers, and, ultimately, for the company that ran the course (to say I caused them some grief would be a gross understatement). After all was said and done, a badly developed course with a poor instructor caused a great deal of problems and ended up costing valuable productivity time not to mention wasted software due to the need to re-design and re-code sections when the truth was later discovered. So, reality is that there are very good courses offered by both large and small companies. There are also very bad ones.

Instructor Qualifications

Now that we have seen how courses are developed, let's consider instructor qualifications for a bit.

I'm a firm believer that experience is the best teacher in the world. While it is true that college has a lot to offer, in the area of network education, most college's curricula leave a great deal to be desired. As a result, many colleges do not have good, solid educational offerings in network subjects and many emphasize the theoretical aspects of networking instead of the practical aspects. Don't get me wrong. I'm not knocking college education. There are some very fine colleges who offer excellent networking courses, but there are usually very difficult to get into and run on a semester basis, something not very conducive to productivity in the workplace. Therefore, most competent networking instructors and consultants I have met have developed their practical competence through the trial and error method and have been smart enough to learn from both their successes and their mistakes as well as those that others have experienced. Through the education through experience path, many things come to light in network education, such as the problems that are not in the documentation, the problems of politics, the problems of dissimilar network software versions on different machines, and many other problems that can be very subtle and very confusing. Anyone can read a manual. Experienced people know this very well. What makes a good networking instructor is one who not only has read the manual, but has had to implement what the manuals say, what they don't say, and also had to violate the rules to get the network to work. There is no substitute for experience. The best networking instructors have a lot of it, know how to teach it to their students, and understand the issues of how to apply it in the real world on real problems.

Some instructors know how to teach, but do not necessarily understand the subject that they are teaching. As a matter of fact, some larger training companies have, historically, hired experienced educators (such as high school teachers) and taught them the subject matter so that they, in turn, could teach the subject to the students who attend the course. This technique can work very well on low-end (introductory) courseware where questions are usually not very complex and are related to the subjects presented. In more technical courses, however, the instructor really needs to be experienced for the students to get the most out of the course that they are attending. In my experience, I often find that students in the more technical courses are attending the course to find out information on the presented subject. Very often, however, they are there to ask very pointed questions about applications and networks they are working on and to draw from the instructor's expertise. If the instructor is not capable of helping the advanced student out, the student usually feels somewhat dissatisfied with the course or feels that the course did not meet the students needs. Both of these will cause the ratings of the course to drop as well as the instructor's teaching ratings. As a result, the course may have been in-line with the course description and may have covered the networking topics described, but such was not done to the satisfaction of the student, therefore the course was not satisfactory as far as the student was concerned. Experience can make the difference, especially in high-end (very technical) courseware, as to whether the course will be successful or not in the eyes of the consumer, the student.

What about Course Content?

Every networking course that is developed has a topic list that is usually included in any marketing literature that is sent out about the course. Things to look for include a clear, thorough outline of course topics to be covered, a brief description of the course (a management-oriented overview), a section that describes **WHAT** will be learned at the course, **PREREQUISITES** for the prospective attendee, **WHO** will be teaching the course, **HOW LONG** the course will last and **HOW MUCH** the course costs. Beware of courses that do not include an outline or do not seem to give a clear idea on what is taught. Also, some courses may have more than one instructor listed but, in the fine print of course, a statement is usually made that not all instructors will be present at each course offering or location. Sometimes, no instructor is listed at all. This is not necessarily bad, but you should check to see who is teaching the course and what their expertise is before attending to insure that you will be satisfied with the instructor and the delivery of the course. I liken course attendance to going to the doctor. I much prefer to go to a doctor who is a specialist when I have a particular problem (such as a sprained ankle) and know who that person is and what kind of experience he/she has so that I can feel confident that I am spending my money properly and getting the best value for my cash. Also, one does not go to an optometrist to get a sprained ankle taken care of. So, specialization helps identify the right individual for the job. Network instructors need to have a wide base of experience, but they should always have an emphasis on networks. Companies that offer network training that are serious networking education companies will offer a variety of networking courses from the introductory level through to the very technical level. This is a good sign as it shows that they are seriously committed to network education and have attacked the network education problem at all levels. It usually can indicate, especially with smaller companies, that there is a good deal of expertise available within the company and that the introductory courses will be just as useful as the technical courses. Companies that provide training in "strings," groups of course offerings from the introductory range in a subject through to the advanced area, are seriously committed to education in that subject and are trying to provide a range of solutions for prospective consumers.

Facilities for network courseware can cause an interesting problem. If you have noticed pricing, network courses tend to be more expensive than "comparable" courses in operating systems or other subjects. This is due to a variety of reasons. To develop networking courses and expertise requires a network (or multiple networks). This means that the cost is much greater, in terms of components necessary, than developing courseware that can be done on a single machine. Networking courses that offer lab sessions cost more because single machine networks are tough to work with and multiple machines, which is what a network consists of, costs a lot more. When looking into network course offerings and a lab is offered, ask questions about the lab conditions and what kind of network resources will be available for learning **AT THE LOCATION YOU WILL BE ATTENDING THE COURSE!!!** Many times brochures can be somewhat misleading. Resources are claimed to be available and are at some locations. Not all networking courses require lab time, but for those that do be sure you understand the facilities that will be available for use. Companies that offer full spectrum course offerings are usually a good bet as they need solid lab facilities to support their offerings. I've attended some networking seminars where the machines were brought in to the hotel where the seminar was being held, so it is quite possible that the claimed facilities will be available. Always check first.

Network courseware costs usually vary according to how many days the course will require to complete, where the course is being held, what facilities are necessary to support the course, how popular the course is, and how much overhead is incurred by the company providing the course. A popular course given by a popular instructor can sometimes be cheaper, as more students will attend each offering, increasing the profitability of the course and lowering the overall cost to the consumers. Low-end courses, such as introductory networking courses, usually last 2-3 days and can cost anywhere from $200.00 to over $2,000.00. Longer courses (3-5 days) can cost up to $5000.00. The more technical the course, the more it will cost. For instance, a five-day intensive introduction course may cost $2000.00, but a five-day internals course can easily cost $3500.00 or much more up to $5000.00 per person per week. Technical courses require a lot more time and expertise to develop, so they tend to be more expensive. They also, typically, do not draw as many students over the life of the course as the low-end courses, and therefore cost more to recoup the development and overhead costs associated with the course.

Some companies that get networks (or will be getting networks) provide in-house education to their employees by contracting with outside educational vendors for courseware. Many times educational courseware vendors provide such courses at a substantial discount to a company because the overall overhead is reduced and a guaranteed student load is realized. Another important point is that travel costs for ten students can be substantial and bringing in a course could usually reduce the cost of education substantially. Many larger companies have known this for years, but smaller companies are starting to realize savings through on-site education as well. There are some other tangible benefits as well. Most of the time, a customer of an education vendor can specify certain topics to be covered and can also, where possible, specify a particular instructor. This can be very useful as many times an experienced instructor can help not only educate a company's employees, but sometimes these instructors may provide customized network education for a given network environment as well as some on-site assistance as the course is being taught. I taught a networking course for a real estate appraisal company about seven years ago, and quickly found out that the network was not even up and running yet and that they were having some serious troubles getting it operational. During breaks and when labs were scheduled, I spent my time working on the network and at the end of the week the students understood the network and it was up and running properly. Looking back on it now, they got a really good deal! I know since then, however, that most reputable and sincerely interested instructors will always spend time working with client companies in trying to help them solve problems that arise during the progress of the course the instructor is delivering. I have one customer that has me teach a four-day course for them on a regular basis and always keeps me the fifth day to help them solve problems that have arisen since my last visit. So, good instructors, when teaching on-site, can provide expertise that is very useful in solving problems during the education process.

Feelin' Satisfied?

Now we have examined how courses are developed, who teaches them, what to look for in literature, facilities issues, and how much they cost. The question that now arises is how do you know which network course you need to satisfy your needs?

The easy answer is that it depends upon your expertise. How you define your expertise will have a lot to do with how satisfied you will be with a seminar choice that you make. I've taught network product internals courses where some people who attended had never seen the product or had never seen a network. While I first thought that it was a fluke, I find that I run into it too often to be an anomaly. Two problems occur when you attend a course which is too advanced for your level of expertise: 1) you will not understand what is being presented to you well enough to make efficient use of what you learn and 2) you will hold up the entire class which hurts everyone involved. Yes, it is true that most people will learn some things of use when they attend a course, no matter how advanced the course is over their level of expertise. It is also true, however, that retention of learned material degrades quickly if the material is not put into use soon after the learning process, so you end up losing most of what you gained, if any gain was made at all. When selecting a course of instruction on networks, be very honest in your self-appraisal of your expertise so that you can properly map the type of courses that you will require for your job. Another thing-never, ever attend more than one course at a time. Attending courses week after week does nothing but slow down the education process and reduce your learning and potential productivity. Always try to attend a course, wait about two months and experiment with the gained knowledge, and attend the next. This will insure maximum productivity for your training expenditure.

Typical Required Network Training

As a general guideline, the following sample job types will require network education as described:

o Department Manager

- Introductory course in networking
- Introductory courses on networking products for which you have responsibility
- Course on understanding network management
- If you control PBX operations, look for the following seminar types:
  - PBX introductory courses
  - PBX planning and sizing
  - Cable management and planning
- Networking trends and technology courses

o Network Manager

- Network product usage courses on networking products for which you have responsibility
- Network management courses on networking products for which you have responsibility
- Network programming courses on networking products for which you have responsibility
- Courses on cable management and planning
- Courses on network troubleshooting and debugging
- Courses on network design and planning
- Network architecture courses
- If you control PBX operations, look for the following seminar types:
  - PBX introductory courses
  - PBX planning and sizing
  - Cable management and planning
  - Specific courses on PBX's in use and under your control:
    o Programming
    o Managing
    o Implementing
    o Expanding
- Networking trends and technology courses

o Network Programmers

- Network product usage courses on networking products for which you have responsibility
- Network programming courses on networking products for which you have responsibility
- Designing applications for networked environments
- Network management conceptual courses
- Network architecture courses

o Network Users

- Introductory course in networking
- Introductory courses on networking products for which you have responsibility
- Network product usage courses on networking products for which you have responsibility
- Courses on how to use applications that have been developed or are in use in your environment

Obviously there are more job types that the above listed ones, but you can get a fairly good idea as the level of education necessary for certain jobs. By the way, the job type of network manager assumes that the network manager already knows quite a bit about networks and the job type of network programmer assumes that the individual is already a competent programmer.

Chapter Summary

Select network training just like you would select a system or any add-on component: carefully, weighing the advantages and disadvantages, and deriving maximum benefit for the cost and energy invested.

Chapter Twelve

Selecting Network Consultants

He who can take advise is sometimes superior to him who can give it.
Karl von Knebel

Introduction

In these days of tight budgets, getting the most for your money, get it done yesterday, fast-paced life of major league computing, the need to get information on the latest, faster and more efficient has become the way of life. We all want to make the "right" decision, but also want to do so in an educated, technically sound way. And, since our bosses think the world of us and know that we will lead them into successful paths of righteousness, we are the anointed few: Design, implement, and manage the new network.

Absolutely. Where do I sign?

Personally, I tend to get seriously concerned when management types start talking about networks. Since the big hoopla about the automated office began, networks have been a big deal as well. At first, management was concerned about office automation, but then they learned all about LOTUS 1-2-3 and figured out all the office automation buzzwords. Hence, they became experts at office automation. Now, as they say in beer commercials, it's network time. That means that management's next area to get involved in is the area of networks. This time, however, the problem is not as easy to solve as integration of a couple of office packages, nor is it as trivial as sticking a modem behind a PC. Don't get me wrong - I'm not slighting office automation. The point I'm illustrating is this: we all know that office automation is not trivial, but it is much easier to handle than the problem of networking; therefore, if management thinks they understand office automation (a lot think that they do), they're in for a BIG shock with networks. Most technical people don't understand networks, so true management enlightenment is still a long way off.

So, how do you find enlightened help in the design, implementation, and management of networks? Or, more simply put, how do you change water into wine?

What is a Network Consultant?

Fear not, help is at hand. There is the elite corps of networking consultants, always eager to help and provide all the answers you need - for a fee, of course. But, before you go off and buy yourself a consultant, let's look into what a networking consultant is and what differentiates him or her from your basic computer consultant.

Networking consultants are a different type of computer consultant. Many computer consultants specialize in a given computer model; operating system, language, application area, or are "generalists" - they know a little about a lot of things. Networking consultants have to be a little different. Not only do they have to understand operating systems, different computing hardware, languages, applications, etc., they also have to understand communications principles, hardware, software, troubleshooting, architecture, design, and many other things that many traditional computer consultants never have to get into. So, in brief, the networking consultant has to understand, in detail, both the hardware and the software of all the systems that the network will touch in addition to the customer's applications problems and business problems. They are hardware engineers, software engineers, architects, field service personnel, programmers, analysts, phone company analysts, and management consultants all wrapped up into one.

The Typical Consultant?

A typical networking consultant will have at least five to 10 years of network design and implementation, usually with multinode (system) networks (yes, Virginia, you can have a single node network) with networks ranging from two to 1,000 or more nodes. An important differentiation to note is that a node is a computer, not necessarily a terminal, printer, or other such "dumb" device. I'll get into why later. Also, networking consultants have exceptional communications skills (if you don't understand what they are trying to tell you, they're not much help), a good understanding of various network architectures, a good understanding of the various domestic and international standards (such as the ISO OSI model, various standards such as X.25, X.3, X.29, X.21, V.35, EIA RS-XXX standards, IEEE standards, ANSI standards, etc.), insights into vendor developments, cable plants and layouts, tech control, network and system management, processor and I/O architecture, problem analysis abilities (if you can't define the problem, you can't solve it), programming experience with several languages (some lend themselves to communications programming better than others), and many other technical capabilities. The networking consultant should also possess the experience of a seasoned computer consultant and have experience with applications design and implementation.

If that weren't enough, the networking consultant should also understand system management, personnel management, budgeting and modeling, expansion analysis, project management, documentation procedures, policy analysis, design, and administration, short and long range planning, vendor interface techniques, and many other management-related skills. You should also consider other items such as educational background, customer base of the consultant (who else has he/she helped), professional society membership, and certifications. Certifications help take a lot of the guesswork out of selection, as the consultant will have had to pass an extensive test, submit credentials for review to a selection board, and, in most cases, sign an ethics statement. At present, there are three technical certifications of interest to anyone considering the hiring of a "certified" professional and all are offered and regulated by the Institute for the Certification of Computer Professionals (ICCP). These certifications are:

o **Certificate in Computer Programming (CCP).** This certification is geared towards professionals with a demonstrated capability in a selected computer language (or languages), programming methods, and other related topics. CCP is considered, usually, the most technical of all certifications but also the most narrow in terms of overall scope.

o **Certificate in Data Processing (CDP).** The CDP certification is a more generalized certification geared towards professionals with a demonstrated capability in various DP related areas such as center management, DP procedures, system architecture, and other topics.

o **Certified Systems Professional (CSP).** Of the three certifications, the CSP is the newest. Started in 1984, the CSP designation was designed for professionals with a broad background in a variety of computer-related disciplines and is comprised of both highly technical and management-oriented topics. Items such as operations research, programming methods, MIS operations, networking, systems architecture, systems analysis, and many other topics comprise the list of requirement for earning the CSP.

In addition to passing a fairly comprehensive test for each certification, each certification requires that all professionals achieving certification re-certify every three years through a plan of demonstrable continuing education in their field or through re-testing. When hiring consultants, certification will become more and more critical as the network marketplace expands and requires that consulting professionals provide a standardized method of submitting credentials for customer approval.

Experience, Experience, oh Wonderful Experience!

In all cases remember that there is no substitute for actual experience; all the academic courses and professional memberships in the world cannot replace being bitten by the network snake. Ask for references and call them for information on the networking consultant you have selected. Remember that you are most likely interrupting their work schedules, so keep your queries short and to the point. Things to ask about would be analytical capabilities (how long it took for the consultant to figure out the problem), quality of work, how long the consultant worked for the customer, would the customer hire the consultant again, and other questions along this vein. Be careful when asking about the nature of work that was done; many customers of consultants cannot discuss the company's networking setup due to corporate policies and, in cases where the final product is being re-sold by the customer, the customer will not wish to discuss it as it may put him in an embarrassing situation. You can find out what you need to make a decision without getting into the architecture of the networks of the consultant's clients.

In a networking environment, the network consultant has the responsibility to his customer to provide the "right" solution, not just "a" solution. And, since the network will eventually touch the customer's business in most facets, the networking consultant has to have the experience and the insight to design and implement the network in a manner that the customer will be able to use and expand without redesigning the network and without incurring unnecessary costs. This usually requires drawing upon the skills in the above paragraph and in the tenacity of the consultant to provide a clear, unbiased solution to the problem at hand.

How to Best Utilize a Network Consultant

Well, we now know what qualifications a networking consultant should have. Let's look at the way you should use networking consultants to get the best mileage out of your consulting budget.

Rule number one in using a consultant: let the consultant HELP you make a decision based upon informed opinion, but, in all cases, make the final call yourself. You will be the one responsible, not the consultant, when everything blows up on Friday night at 5:00. If you let the consultant make your decisions for you, you can rest assured that you will be disappointed at some time or another. There are many consulting types in the marketplace, but truly enlightened consultants know better than to make decisions for the customer for a couple of reasons: the customer has to be comfortable in his decision to be satisfied with the implementation, and a consultant's role is NOT to make decisions; the consultant is there to present workable alternatives and give educated opinions based upon previous experience and understanding of the customer's needs. I've always told consultants that unless they can come up with at least three different ways to solve the same problem, they're not doing their jobs. Having the necessity of choice allows the customer to choose the "right" way to do the job based upon the business needs of the company, which the customer will always understand better than the consultant.

Don't Think You Can Do It All

Rule number two in choosing a networking consultant: don't think that you can do it all yourself. You wouldn't be thinking about hiring a consultant if you could. Many times, consultants will recommend actions that may seem like a waste of time to you, but, in reality, are very necessary. A group I was involved with recently wanted to put in a very large network with PCs and systems scattered all over the western hemisphere. What they wanted was to do most of it themselves and have me provide guidance for them, which was fine. But, when it came time to look at the cost matrix and traffic matrix and compute both for the first phase of the network, they felt that the matrix computations were unnecessary because they weren't sure what the growth would be. I tried to convince them otherwise, but they did not want to hear anything other than their own words. At that point, I gave them their money back and walked away form the project. The reasons? Computation of the traffic matrix (how much data from what node to what node and how often for all nodes on the network) is critical to network design because it will dictate how much data can be shoved through the network before the performance dies. It also shows the load factors on the systems on the network that will be accessing the data involved. The traffic matrix also shows how much expansion room will be available and how long the current design will last before it has to be subdivided, enhanced, or replaced with a better design architecture. Second, the cost matrix is important as it will dictate how much money will be necessary to transfer data between nodes and also useful in setting up the least cost path between nodes. So, without these two factors being computed, it is virtually impossible to wave the rubber chicken at the network and declare it functional and wonderful.

While it is true that they may not have known what they would be expanding to, they did know what they currently had and could have set up a base from which to work. If you know the basic capabilities, you will also know how much you can expand before you have to do a major overhaul on the network. Also, if you have some idea as to how fast the business will expand (you can find this out through a historical perspective on the company's business), you can estimate how long it will be before the network reaches critical mass and something will have to be done. Therefore, how extensive a network will be or how much data it can/will handle is directly dependent upon a good estimate of traffic load and plugging in cost numbers.

What Can a Consultant Provide?

A good consultant provides conservative, truthful answers to problems based upon actual, factual information, not rumors, estimates, or heresay that cannot be substantiated with facts. So, it may look like magic, but it isn't. Use the consultant for the hard stuff, have him suggest things that you can do on your own (to save you money and time), and remember that he is the person you hired because of his knowledge. Use it!

Good Consultants Are Truthful Consultants

Rule number three in selecting a networking consultant: a good consultant will always tell you the truth, no matter how unpalatable it may be. It is better to know what is real and will work than implement something that sounds good but won't. An experienced networking consultant will be able to help you differentiate between real and unreal and will not hesitate to point out the differences. If you know what is real, your disappointments will be few and your successes many.

Complexity is Better Than How Many Nodes

Rule number four in selecting a networking consultant: the complexity involved in network designs the consultant has worked on are much more desirable than how many nodes. I've seen consultants who claimed 100 node networks and, after some research, the "network" turned out to be 100 terminals with 1200 baud modems dialed-up to a system, playing dumb terminals. That's distributed processing, which is not the same as networking. I'd rather use a consultant who has had to configure a network with local area linkages (such as Ethernet), configuration of routing nodes, gateways (to X.25, SNA and others), internets, repeaters, and other such items. That kind of practical experience with difficult connectivity problems is much more useful than how many nodes someone has hooked up to a wire or how many dial-ups there are on a computer.

Network Management is a Must

Rule number five in selecting a networking consultant: look for experience in network use and management. Many consultants are quick to configure a network, but few have practical, daily experience in running a network and providing technical control and support of network resources. This is a critical item because management of a network leads to empathy with the customer - the problem is seen from the customer's side as the consultant has been there before. There are some real problems in the support area of the network that have to be experienced to be believed, so look for a consultant with direct control experience. I always liken this item to the problem of dealing with vendor engineering. When I worked for a major computer vendor, I can remember producing solutions and software that were sound from an engineering standpoint, but the customers sometimes gave me grief because it was "not enough" or "too difficult to use" or, worse yet, they "didn't need all the features." As a consultant, I had a hard time figuring out what they wanted. However, when I was a customer in the same predicament, I understood immediately what it was they were talking about. Just because the engineering expertise is sound does not mean that a consultant understands all the aspects of the solution. Also, a good consultant is not afraid to bring in other help when out of his or her league. This means that it is much better to find a consultant who uses other personnel with different expertise than one who tries to do it alone. There is safety in numbers when it comes to design, and use of a knowledge base rather than a single individual increases the likelihood of a superior solution.

How Much Does a Consultant Cost?

Since you have found the ultimate consultant and are now ready to wage war on the network problem that has been confronting you; the question of the hour comes up: how much do networking consultants cost? Well, they ain't cheap.

Typical consulting rates for networking consultants usually run about 20-40 percent higher than comparable rates for straight computer consultants. Some rates are as low as $35 an hour and you can expect to pay as much as $250 an hour for top folks working on difficult problems. Some consulting firms charge flat rates per day ($500-$2,500 a day) and can also quote flat rates for projects that have been well defined. Remember, in all cases, you get what you pay for. You may pay $150 an hour for a top consultant, but you may only need him for a couple of weeks whereas you may pay $50 an hour for a less experienced consultant and end up using him for two months. That is not to say that less expensive consultants are not as experienced, but most top consultants are in demand because of their experience and charge higher prices accordingly. Overall, if you consider the fact that a bad network put together without proper design can cost up to five times more to fix or replace than a properly designed and implemented network, the price of a good consultant is cheap. By the way, if you find a good networking consultant, hang on to him. They're not that easy to find.

Where Can You Find One?

When looking for a good consultant, there aren't many places to go for information, but there are some. User groups are good place to start. Yes, I know that many user groups are supposed to be non-commercial, but users will be users. Asking other user group members at local and national meetings can be a good way to find good consultants. Another method is to contact companies with networks and ask their networking managers for names of consultants. Vendors are usually a help in finding consultants as well, but beware: they will usually try to sell you their own personnel. Finally, contact professional computer membership organizations for help; they usually can provide names through a referral service or membership roster.

Chapter Summary

Be selective in choosing a network consultant and remember, they can be very helpful in the design, implementation, and management of your network. It's like the old business adage, "to make money, you have to spend money."

Choose a consultant with a good track record, one you feel you can trust. And, always beware of the definition of GURU:

"Good Understanding, but Relatively Useless."

Chapter Thirteen

Ethernet Implementation
Case Studies

There are many truths of which the full meaning cannot be realized until personal experience has brought it home.

John Stuart Mill

Introduction

Ethernet is not like many other types of networks. While it can solve a great many networking problems, there are a great many issues to consider when designing and implementing a network. As such, this chapter is devoted to looking a few implementations of Ethernet as a demonstration of Ethernet's versatility and capabilities.

Case One: The Bank

In the first example, the customer is a medium sized bank (about $25 billion in assets) who had the following requirements:

o Connect various IBM PCs on various floors to a VAXCluster system
o Provide connectivity to various laser printers
o Provide a shared storage environment between PCs
o Allow for growth and ease of reconfiguration

While there are a great many types of networks that would fulfill the needs, Ethernet was chosen due to its flexibility and software availability. Another reason for choice was the ready availability of Ethernet connectivity hardware for the VAXCluster systems and the PCs.

To facilitate the installation of the PCs a standard PC configuration was chosen to provide a known network environment on each PC. Since the PCs needed to communicate more with each other than with the VAX systems, emphasis was placed on connectivity software at the PC level with a secondary emphasis on software for connection to the VAX systems.

After some research, it was decided that the 3Com Etherseries of hardware and software would provide the necessary PC-to-PC connectivity by allowing disk sharing, printer sharing to connected printers on the Ethernet as well as a generic connectivity method for future PCs, such as Apple Macintoshes, as they became available. This choice turned out to be very functional for the VAX connectivity as well as a package known as VIM (VAX Interface Manager) was placed on the VAX systems to allow VAX systems to work with the 3Com software. Through the use of VIM, PC users could connect to the VAX as virtual terminals (allowing interactive usage of the system) as well as being able to provide disk server capabilities by generating messages and protocol emulating a 3Com disk server. The 3Com software on the PCs throught that they were connected to a disk server; in reality, they were using a virtual disk on a VAX as if the virtual disk were an actual disk server. Through this trickery, a PC user could now share disk resources, files, software, models, and many other desirable items. Also, the virtual disks (being VAX files) could easily be backed-up for the users by the system manager/operators utilizing the VMS BACKUP utility, greatly simplifying network and system management both on the PCs and the VAXCluster system. Through the usage of the EBRIDGE utility on the VAX systems, VAX files could be created from the contents of the virtual disks. Also insertion of VAX files into the virtual disks was now possible.

It was decided that a thinwire (RG58 R/U cable) Ethernet would be used to connect the 3Com Ethernet controllers in the PCs to the network. As with most PC controllers, the 3Com controller is capable of supporting the thinwire by setting DIP switches on the controller so that the controller card not only supplies controller services, but also supplies transceiver services as well. This means that to hook up a PC to the network, all the network manager need do is connect the PC to the thinwire cable with a BNC twist-and-lock connector in a "T" fashion. Since the 3Com controller allows the transceiver circuitry to be enabled or disabled (depending upon switch settings), the PCs could be directly connected to the network without having to use an external transceiver. In the few cases where the PCs were not located near the thinwire network sections, the PCs were connected to the thickwire Ethernet by using external H4000 transceiver (made by DEC) or 3Com transceiver by tapping the thickwire, installing the transceiver, and using a 15-wire transceiver cable from the transceiver to the 3Com controller in the PC. On the back of the controller is both the BNC connector and a connector suitable for a 15-pin transceiver cable, allowing the same controller to function in both the thinwire and thickwire environment.

VAX systems were connected to the Ethernet utilizing DELUA UNIBUS Ethernet adapters, the VMS Ethernet Class Driver software (it comes with VMS - XEDRIVER.EXE), the Ethernet Ring Buffer Driver (ESDRIVER.EXE), and the VIM software package that connects to the Ethernet class driver. As the VAX systems adapter does not have an on-board transceiver capability, external adapters are required (in this case, the H4000 transceiver). Through this configuration, the VAX systems were able to freely communicate with the PCs and vice-versa.

The only other stumbling block to the installation was the connection of the thinwire segment to the thickwire segment. In most installations, the thinwire segment would

136

be attached to the thickwire segment through a special device known as a repeater. The function of a repeater is to connect two Ethernet segments together, making both segments appear as a single segment to all system connected. In this case, the network was implemented before such repeaters were readily available, so it was decided to directly connect the thickwire to the thinwire utilizing a barrel connector between the two segments. The problem with this type of connection scheme is twofold: a) the overall length and noise attenuation restrictions change and b) if a user disconnects a PC from the network improperly, he/she may leave the network in an open-short state, effectively neutralizing the entire network (Ethernets either work or do not work; there is no in-between). The length restriction and noise issues become a problem as whenever two cables of different basic electrical properties become connected, the properties of both cable change. The problem also illustrates the problems of mixed-cable types. For instance, if the overall Ethernet were 100% thickwire, the cable would have a maximum length restriction of 500 meters. If the cable were all thinwire, it would realize a maximum length of 189 meters. Combine the two, and things get strange. For instance, if the Ethernet configuration were 75% thickwire and 25% thinwire, the length tolerance would be completely different than the situation where the Ethernet were 75% thinwire and 25% thickwire. Get the point? It's not as easy as it looks when mixed cable types are involved. In this case, the cable is 60% thickwire and 40% thinwire with a total cable length of 210 meters, which works nicely. The most common problem with the mixed cable type is the second problem mentioned: users improperly disconnecting the cable from the PCs when the PCs are removed from the workspaces.

The "T" connector on the back of the PCs is basically a female connector to the PC (a male connector is typically on the back of PC controllers) with two male connectors that "T" into the thinwire cable as it runs behind the PC. The logical and preferred way to disconnect the cable is by disconnecting the female connector from the male connector on the back of the controller in the PC. Since this is usually difficult for the user to get to, users tend to disconnect the two female connectors on the cable ends rather than disconnecting the one female connector to the PC controller. The effect is quite clear and immediate: the network connection is "broken" and the entire network fails. The only way to find the fault is to either systematically search each potential location of connection and place a connector between the disconnected pieces or to place a device called a Time Domain Reflectometer (TDR) at one end of the cable to ascertain where the break is located. A TDR sends an electrical signal down the wire and waits for the reflection of the signal. If no reflection is received (the cable is "infinitely" long), the there is no break. If, however, the TDR showed a reflection at 55 meters, that is where the break has occurred. In this case, a TDR was not always readily available so usually a terminator is placed at strategic points on the cable until a particular section of the thinwire segment is isolated as having the breakage. While tedious, it does work and precludes the need to go from cubicle to cubicle trying to figure out which PC is missing.

So, the real question is now: how well has Ethernet proven itself to do the job?

The aforedescribed network was installed in 1985 and has proven itself to be very reliable and functional. The only major problem is when users decide to disconnect their

137

systems from the network to take them home or other such disruption. By educating the users to the hazards of disconnection as well as placing plastic covers on the network BNC connections, user disruptions are limited to about two to three a month and are usually fixed within 30 minutes. Since critical uptime is not a requirement, the 30-minute break determination time is usually sufficient and the customer has been very pleased with the connectivity and results.

The Office Building

In another case, a 10 story office building owned by a large oil company had a need to distribute computing power to various floors as well as allow terminal connectivity to the distributed systems. As the customer primarily relied upon DEC systems for computational power, Ethernet hookups were easily accomplished. The problem was how to get all the terminals hooked up and also provide a solid reliable network. In this application, network availability was critical for certain applications and downtime could not be tolerated.

In the initial network design, the customer tried to design the network themselves. In a classic style, the customer configured the network in such a fashion as a backbone

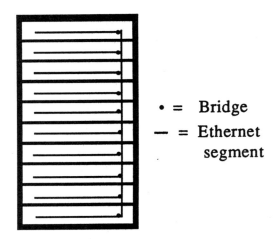

• = Bridge

— = Ethernet
    segment

Original Customer Design

Ethernet ran the distance of the building (through the telephone closets on one side of the building) with each floor running a separate segment of Ethernet and connected to the backbone through an Ethernet bridge. A bridge is similar in nature to a repeater except that the bridge does not repeat all traffic from one segment to another. Rather, the bridge "learns" which node is one which segment and only forwards traffic to a remote segment when there is traffic actually destined for a node on the remote segment. If the traffic is between nodes on the same segment, it does not propagate traffic to other segments. While the initial approach works and provides the desired connectivity, the reliability became an issue. Since the backbone ran the entire distance of the building, the network backbone became an exposed entity and was the subject of frequent disruptions as workers in telephone closets accidentally cut or disrupted the cable on a regular ba-

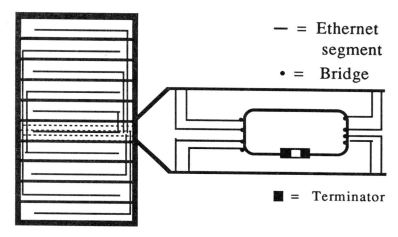

— = Ethernet
segment

• = Bridge

■ = Terminator

Enhanced Network Design

sis.

To solve the problems of the backbone as well as allow expansion, a separate wire center was established near the computer room. A segment of Ethernet cable was strung around the room in a spiral to form the backbone and all floor's segments terminated in the room. From the ends of the various floor segments, repeaters were attached to the backbone spiral, effectively giving a backbone network but keeping the entire backbone in a single room where it could be protected, monitored, and enhanced. In this manner, all segments could be controlled from one spot and the backbone was protected. As an additional precaution, every other floor's segment was run on the opposite side of the building to keep the segments from all being knocked out by a catastrophe in a single closet on a particular floor.

A side benefit from this scheme was the ability to dynamically reconfigure, manually, the network in case of failure. By making the backbone of such a length that its length plus the length of any particular segment would not exceed 500 meters total length, the network manager may directly connect the backbone to any other segment with a barrel connector at the end of the backbone and the segment to allow the network to bypass an errant repeater or bridge. This feature allows emergency reconfiguration of the network on an on-demand basis and allows rapid isolation of faulty components.

To solve the terminal connectivity problem, DEC terminal servers were selected to allow terminals to connect to the Ethernet and allow the connected servers to connect to existing DEC machines on the network. A terminal server is basically either a PDP-11/24 (DECSA box) or MC68000 (DSRVx DECServer box) system that serves the functions of a multiplexer for terminal traffic destined for a particular host system such as a VAX or PDP-11. In some cases, the terminal servers themselves may function as a host by providing what is called "reverse LAT" services. In this configuration, a terminal server allows incoming connections to be made and connects the sessions to the asynchronous ports on the server. This configuration is highly useful where systems such as IBM and Data General systems cannot directly connect to the Ethernet, but their asynch ports may be accessible by connecting the systems to a terminal server and allowing the terminal server to provide the host connectivity functions.

In the normal installation of the terminal servers, certain VAX systems on the network were selected as "load hosts" to provide operating system loading services to the terminal servers. Terminal servers do not have any directly attached load media (such as a disk drive or tape drive) and do not have the terminal server kernel in ROM as other systems may. As a result, the operating system for the terminal server must be loaded into the server from a host system so that the server will function. DECnet communications software provides the necessary loading services for the terminal servers, so configuration proved to be fairly simple. DEC includes appropriate configuration software to allow the network manager to set up the server requests properly on the host systems and allow the host systems to respond promptly to server load requests.

What is the Status of the Network?

Installed in 1984, the network now has over 60 VAX systems installed on it and over 100 terminal servers providing connectivity services for over 800 terminals. The servers have proven to be reliable and functional and allow the terminals good throughput and high availability. Network availability was improved markedly by the minor redesign of the backbone and now experiences less than 2% downtime per year, most of that being scheduled.

The Factory

This case involved a factory which makes glass for use in various commercial and industrial products. In this situation, a network was required that would provide connectivity between existing machines on the factory floor and new systems that would be implemented at a later date to automate certain factory functions.

Factory networks require some special considerations that are not usually required with office networks. While it is quite true that the main intent of many Ethernets is to pro-

140

vide office systems and machine connectivity, it has been determined that properly configured Ethernets are quite capable of functioning well in the industrial and factory environments as well.

One of the main stumbling points with many factory and process control networks is the problem of providing absolute response times for certain processes in progress on the floor. For example, the need to control a chemical reaction requires that the system and the network exhibit a known response time frequency. It would not do at all for a reaction to be at a critical point in the chain and the system not react fast enough to inject a stabilizing agent into a chemical mixture or open up coolant valves to cool down a mixture. As a result, factory and process networks require special care and "feeding" when it comes to network technology.

Ethernet is what is known as a "statistical" network. This means that the network cable is always available for access, from a physical point of view, but the network may be unavailable for access at any given moment if some other station is using the network. How often a node may "grab" the Ethernet medium is directly dependent upon a lot of different issues: average length of messages being transmitted, number of message being transmitted, time of the day, number of network-available nodes on the network, types of imbedded protocols being used, and many other issues. In all situations, it is statistically possible to provide that a node will generally be able to access the Ethernet within a certain time window, depending upon the listed factors. The problem is that certain types of functions, such as catalytic reactions, do not understand the problems of statistical networks and may require immediate gratification: the network HAS to be available NOW!

Many companies that sell networks to the process control and factory environments tend to push the concept of token-passing networks. A token-passing network is one that uses a virtual structure known as a token and passes information from node to node in the token. It's like the old fire brigades where a line of men would assemble and pass water from man to man in buckets until it got to its destination - the fire. The reason this type of network is flaunted in the process environment (especially) is because of the predictive property of the network. A token-passing network is often referred to as deterministic because nodes (systems) on the network KNOW when they will be receiving the token based upon traffic load, number of nodes, etc... A network designer can predict, fairly accurately, the arrival distribution of empty tokens to a particular node and predict, again fairly accurately, when the destination node will receive the token with the transmitted information in it. Because of this, process and factory networks can be configured in such a fashion as to control processes that require a predictable and reliable response time.

Because the network hardware provides a deterministic arrival distribution, many companies in the process control area leap on the token-passing bandwagon. The problem is that most companies forget one crucial issue involved: the hardware may be deterministic, but the network response is also a function of the software and the host systems, which are frequently statistical in nature.

Modern multiprocessing (or multitasking) computing systems depend upon scheduling algorithms to provide the multiprocessing capabilities on a single CPU. As such, the system is not dedicated to a particular function and must share time with all system functions and programs. Such scheduling is done in a variety of methods on different operating systems, but most process systems utilize vendor-supported operating systems which are, very frequently, general purpose in nature and do not provide predictable, consistent response times for on-going jobs, much less the statistical queueing properties of network queues. As a result, the network hardware may be deterministic in nature, but frequently the network and operating system software is not that which causes the response time intervals at each system to be statistical. Statistical not based upon the network; statistical based upon each systems scheduling and network access software.

Bottom line? Token-passing mechanisms may provide a deterministic approach to a network plan, but often the software may throw out any illusion of deterministic response. Since Ethernet is statistical in nature, some studies have shown that with the proper loading metrics and packet sizes, an Ethernet is more reliable from a packet arrival determination point of view than many deterministically oriented networks.

Why go into this digression? Because it is important to know that Ethernet is not only capable of office networking, but also that it can be used in areas where deterministic networks roam. Also, it is important to note that in some situations, Ethernet may provide better response time and easier installation and reliability than some token passing schemes. Not to put down token passing schemes, mind you. No, more to make the point that for a network to be truly deterministic and provide a truly deterministic response, it is important that all components of the network be deterministic in nature.

Back to the factory network. The customer felt that the usage of an Ethernet was warranted, as the network would not be used for absolute real-time response issues, but, rather, for updates, system loads, and other such functions that do not require the network to respond in an instantaneous fashion. Additionally, the network is scheduled for some serious growth, and Ethernet could easily handle the growth and allow all systems, factory and proposed office automation systems, to happily co-exist on the same network.

One of the first issues with the Ethernet layout was the running of the backbone thick-wire cable. While this usually does not present a major problem in a building, in a factory it may. In some factories, very large AC or DC motors may exist that generate serious radio frequency (RF) or electromagnetic (EM) interference. Such interference could wreak havoc on an improperly grounded or shielded Ethernet, so it is best to configure the cable plant in such a manner as to avoid such locations and try to keep taps and connectors clear of areas that could present an interference hazard. This is done by carefully noting such locations on an electrical wiring diagram and by running cable away from such locations in shielded cable trays, conduit, or other such EM and RF dampening environments. While this may seem trivial, it is not. Ethernets are very sensitive to off-frequency noise, especially when the Ethernet cable starts exceeding 117 meters. By properly shielding cable areas and keeping a clean ground on the Ethernet cable, the network is assured of good response with minimal interference.

Following the cable issues are the problems of cable access. Many factory environments provide cable trays high above the floor so that electrical service areas and other wiring centers are easily accessed. This also means that taps may materialize on the Ethernet cables in such wireways and may be subjected to harsh environments (like extreme heat near a blast furnace, such as one used to melt down the components for glass), corrosive materials, and other unwholesome issues. Another problem is restriction of access to the cable by factory personnel. Many factories are very safe to work in, but industrial accidents do happen. If a fork truck were to rip open a wire duct, the network could easily be knocked out and it could take some time to repair. Other hazards such as disgruntled employees have been known to cause network cable problems at very inopportune times if the cable is too accessible. Protection of the network cable plant is extremely important in the factory environment as it may be very difficult to access the cable plant or even to locate the specific point of the break.

As such, it was determined that the Ethernet to be used in the factory would be divided into multiple Ethernet segments and bridge interconnect boxes would be used to connect the segments together. This has two effects. First, the network is segmented, so should one Ethernet segment fail, the remaining segments could easily continue to operate. Second, traffic that is on a particular segment will not be propagated to the other segments unless the traffic is actually destined to go to a particular node (or set of nodes) on a remotely connected segment. Both features are desirable qualities on a factory network.

Connection of the systems in the factory turned out to be fairly easily to do. Since all the systems were DEC PDP-11 and VAX systems, controller and software were easily found and installed. The most flagrant problem was the installation of the networking software on the PDP-11/73 systems.

The PDP-11/73 system is a reincarnation of the older PDP- 11/70 system on a smaller chassis with a different I/O bus structure. In the factory environments, the customer had chosen to run RSX-11M/Plus, a multitasking operating system that is very popular in the DEC PDP environment. While RSX- 11M/Plus does a respectable job at generalized and some realtime computing, the networking software caused other problems that were not adequately planned for by the customer.

143

RSX-11M/Plus uses a section of memory to contain the operating system executive and a storage area known as the dynamic storage region (referred to as POOL). The POOL area in the executive code+data area is a fixed size and requires that a great many items be stored in it. It is a kind of system scratch pad that gets used on a regular basis for volatile structures and software that is required for system performance.

When the network software was installed on the system, the kernel code for the network package requires that a section of the executive code+data space be used to store the network executive. This obviously has an effect on the POOL. Since the code+data space is of a restricted size, the inclusion of additional code in the space (the network software) causes the POOL size to decrease, dramatically. The end effect is that where everything used to fit in the POOL, now there is a very tight squeeze. To compound the problem, the network software also causes the POOL to be consumed by the network executive for storage of volatile structures. End effect? POOL, under load situations, becomes rapidly depleted, and the system crashes. The cause is the additional load on the POOL in addition to the reduction of POOL size caused by installation of the network software. The effect is that the systems fail, on a semi-regular basis, and they did not fail previous to the installation of the Ethernet and the networking software.

In this case, the problem is difficult to fix easily. It was fixed by re-generating the operating system and reducing the size of the operating system executive to only the code+data required to fulfill the function of the configured system. This frees up additional space in the executive+data fixed area and allows more to be allocated to POOL. It also helped stop the spurious system crashes and the systems continued to compute properly.

End Result?

The network has been running successfully since early 1986 and the customer plans on implementing an additional 10 superminicomputers to support the additional factory functions. The initial problems with the software corrected on the PDP-11 systems caused a great leap in confidence on the part of management and a full-factory Ethernet has been installed, tested, and implemented.

Chapter Summary

Implementation of Ethernets varies from application to application. Depending upon the different needs of the applications involved, the network configuration may need to be modified to fit.

Network configuration is not a trivial thing. In this chapter we have explored some sample implementations and given a basic synopsis of SOME of the issues involved. These solutions are not all-inclusive and have certainly evolved over time - and will continue to do so. Any design requires the considerations mentioned in previous chapters as well as a meld between the political and esoteric needs of the company. Never overlook the details; seemingly minor issues can flare up and cause serious long-term problems.

Finally, network implementations can be done well if thought and consideration are carefully included in the design. Snap designs frequently have other related problems and can end up costing more than a good design and implementation would have from the inception.

Chapter Fourteen

Ethernet and the Future

The future is not a problem to be solved, it is an experience to enjoy.
                                                        Marvin A. Davis

Introduction

Where a technology has come from is important. Where a technology is going is equally, if not more, important as it dictates whether or not a good decision has been made in regard to the choice and usage of the technology. In this chapter, we will look at some potential developments and try to illuminate the 'ole crystal ball for some insight into possible future developments.

Ground Rules

In any type of forecasting or prognostication, there have to be some ground rules. After all, if there were no caveats, disclaimers or "don't blame me's," how could you take anyone's predictions seriously?

Well, this book is no different. To properly put the issue of futures and predictions in perspective, I will quote Bill's First Law of Networks:

"Never believe anything until it is obsolete. And then hold on to your doubts."

Through application of this law, you will never be taken advantage of and will never have to worry about vendor claims of glory and speed.

In all seriousness, it is fairly impossible to predict the actual outcome of the impact of Ethernet on the networking marketplace and how it will finally be looked upon in years to come. It is fair to say, however, that with minor modifications to the concepts of Ethernet, a number of products centering around the conceptual technology will emerge in the next few years and they, in turn, will lead to other types of developments that derive their roots from Ethernet.

Always remember, however, that it is fun to prognosticate and imagine about the future. It is a different thing entirely to base corporate decisions upon possible future technologies, so DON'T DO IT!! Looking into a two- year time frame is very useful. Looking to a five-year time frame is about as carried away as one would want to get.

Chances are very good that even in five years, Ethernet will "look" somewhat different than today and anything put into place today will most likely require some sort of lobotomy to work properly with future network developments.

Bottom line? Buy what works; buy what is available now and in the very short term. Never base corporate plans on network technologies that are, essentially, "vaporware." Make your motto "Deeds, not words." Tell vendors to put up or shut up. In short, look to the future, but don't bet the house on it.

Deterministic Ethernet

As previously discussed, one of the problems with Ethernet from the process control side of computing is that there is a general complaint that Ethernet does not provide a method to guarantee that a station will respond within a certain time frame. To compound the issue, there is no way to guarantee that a node will be able to access the communications channel in a certain time frame that may be required for functions required in real-time or process-driven environments. Some customers of Ethernet have taken the claims of lack of being able to determine the response to a station and implemented networks show that the lack of response is not worth worrying about. Other, more cautious to, companies have taken the tack that token ring support is required due to its deterministic nature and that Ethernet's basic statistical access method will never measure up. In any case, the battle over Ethernet in environments that require a certain response time rages on and will most likely not be decided for some time.

Most network engineers agree that in the case of control of critical real-time processes, the potential of a statistical network delaying critical component communication is real. In the real world, however, very few actual instrumentation packages are directly connected to a network; most are connected to a computer which, in turn, is connected to a network. If the network is lightly loaded, concern over when a node can get data on the network on an Ethernet is somewhat moot. The fear of the network locking up under a heavy load is very real and quite probable. So, Ethernets can work well in areas where deterministic networks roam, provided they are lightly loaded or under very strict control. Unfortunately, this cannot be guaranteed, and delays could still occur. So the problem is: how does one get Ethernet to react in a predictable manner without causing major architectural problems in the process?

That was the issue at hand for the French Institut National de Recherche en Informatique et en Automatique (also known as INRIA). The INRIA was asked by the French Navy to provide a network architecture for future battleships that would be robust, flexible, and based upon mature technology. While Ethernet fits the bill nicely, the problem is that in a military environment, messages MUST be delivered in a certain predictable time frame or the network is useless. Tactical control situations require high volumes of traffic be transmitted and received in a very short amount of time and in a predictable, stable manner. Ethernets begin to exhibit fairly unstable characteristics as the network traffic becomes more bursty and heavy, a situation that is intolerable for military purposes. It is even worse if there are retransmissions involved due to collisions: a station may try up to 16 times before the packet gets out of the node, if it does at all. On larger Ethernets, it can take up to 52 microseconds to detect a collision, which is unacceptable for required-response networks.

To solve the problem, the French team used a fairly common database technique, a binary search tree, to replace the traditional Ethernet backoff and retry algorithm. By mapping nodes on the network with information about the network and forcing certain nodes to back off and others to send (in accordance with algorithmic rules) at regular retry intervals, a predictable delivery time can be provided to all stations. This feature allows Ethernet technology to be used in areas where deterministic networks are required due to response time, and yet preserves the high-speed nature and multi-node access of traditional Ethernet.

One of the best features of the technology is that it is basically plug-compatible with existing chips used on controllers that access Ethernet. Changeout of the chips would be in the range of $45.00 and would be plug-compatible with existing Ethernet controller chip sets. As a result, companies that require a deterministic method of accessing Ethernet could upgrade to the modified network for substantially less than it would take to install a broadband network (for, say, MAP) or to parallel-install token ring networks to provide the deterministic facility for process and factory control while retaining Ethernet for office and corporate functions.

Ethernet Backbones

A quiet but important network has been under standardization development for some time. Called the Fiber Distributed Data Interface (FDDI) Network, it is being developed by ANSI X3T9.5 and the IEEE 802 committee as a high-speed interconnect between systems and other 802 series networks (such as 802.3 - Ethernet and 802.5 - token ring).

The FDDI looks somewhat similar in structure to the 802.5 token-passing-ring architecture. In fact, some of the architectural considerations are modeled after it. But, that is about as far as it goes. In application, the FDDI has superior speed, redundancy, and length capabilities. It is a 100Mbit/sec fiber-based network that can be stretched over a distance of about 200 kilometers (124 miles). While the standard does not prescribe a given number of nodes on the network, nor a specific separation distance between nodes, at present it is estimated that the network could handle 1,000 nodes attached to it. This allows tuning of the network for specific applications and configurations, thus increasing its flexibility. But there is more.

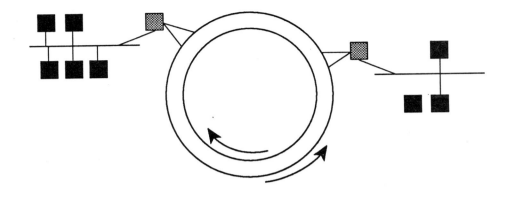

FDDI Ring Topology

FDDI is also unique from 802.5 in that it specifies the usage of not one 100Mbit ring, but two. The rings transmit light in opposite directions and work in tandem with each other, allowing reconfiguration in case of failure of one of the rings and, in some situations, the ability for certain applications to use both rings simultaneously for an aggregate throughput of 200Mbit/sec. While the concept of dual ring networks is not new, the usage of the architecture with fiber is. The choice of fiber was obvious:

1. Fiber has a high degree of security. The only way to connect to fiber is to cut the fiber. Also, fiber does not radiate electrical or magnetic noise, making it virtually impervious to electronic eavesdropping or other such data gathering techniques.

2. Noise immunity. Because the fiber is either glass or, in some cases, high-grade plastic, it is insensitive to the noise and distortions normally caused to networks by machines, AC and DC motors, and many other industrial and commercial machines. As such, fiber is a very desirable medium for usage in high-electrical and magnetic noise environments such as factories.

3. Low attenuation. Many cable plants continue to degrade the electrical signature of a signal being transmitted as the signal proceeds down the cable path. Not so with fiber. After the first few meters the signal has attenuated all that it is going to, so there is not the problem of continuing signal degradation experienced with copper coax and the like. While it is true that the connectors for attaching nodes to fiber introduce noise, new connector technologies have been quite successful in reducing signal loss to 2db or less.

4. Available bandwidth. Fiber has an almost unlimited available bandwidth and transmission speed is usually not limited by the fiber but by the cost to provide transmission and reception facilities that are fast enough to make optimal use of the medium.

While 200Mbits may seem fast, some fiber plants are quite capable of handling over 3.75THz (tera (trillion) Hertz) of bandwidth. AT&T has been successful in demonstrating network data transmissions in excess of 20Gbits over a single fiber of the type used in most average fiber installations today. This provides for the usage of the same medium for a long period of time without having to replace the medium. If a higher speed network is desired, simply replace the transmitting and receiving equipment, not the "cable."

In short, FDDI is fast, efficient, and a standard. It is also compliant with the 802.2 Medium Access Control (MAC) specification. This allows the network to be used as a backbone to other 802 series of networks such as the 802.3, 802.4 (token bus) and 802.5. With this type of interplay, any 802-compliant network may be able to exchange data with any other 802-compliant network. This can be especially useful where 802.5 token rings exist in a factory and connection to office facilities on an 802.3 is desired.

Another by-product of the specification is the ability to hook up nodes that are not necessarily other 802 networks. There is no reason that devices such as terminal cluster controllers, tape controllers, and disks could not be connected to the medium and allowed to be accessed. This presents some interesting options to computer vendors. Disks could be located in one building, processors in another, and users at terminals located in still other locations, all connected together and happily networking together. Because of the distances allowed by FDDI, there is no longer any reason that main system components need to be geographically co-located. In fact, already some vendors have produced suitable VLSI chipsets for FDDI interconnection (consisting of a receiver, transmitter, media access controller, data path controller, and node buffer memory chips) on controller boards. This simplifies the problems of access as now existing network controller and other types of device controllers will be able to connect to the FDDI network without a great deal of effort involved.

While FDDI is fast, it lacks certain attributes required to make it useful for voice and data transmission. To handle this, a modified version of FDDI, called FDDI II, is being proposed to handle the voice/data problem. One signalling channel of 1.024Mbit/s is specified as well as 16 dynamically programmable channels of 6.144Mbit/s. Since the basic framework of FDDI also allows for a slotted (insertion) ring, the needs of voice transmission are satisfied. Voice usually requires some sort of deterministic transmission method, either a circuit-switched link or a time division multiplexed (TDM) link mechanism. Slotted rings are usually considered to provide the TDM facility, therefore FDDI can supply voice transmission services in a generally accepted manner.

In summary, FDDI is an important standard to Ethernet. At present, Ethernets may be interconnected via local or remote bridge networks. The possibility of a backbone, however, causes throughput problems and creates propagation delay issues that are not easily solved. By the use of an FDDI backbone, Ethernets may be easily interconnected and used with other Ethernets or series 802 networks.

Ethernet Hubs

Some companies have discovered that Ethernet is not the cure to all problems. Big surprise! In some situations, however, Ethernet is a good solution, but because of building or network layout one type of cable does not solve all the Ethernet problems.

Most corporate environments considering usage of Ethernet find quickly that thickwire Ethernet is somewhat inflexible and imposes configuration problems that may be unsurmountable for certain types of applications. The use of thinwire is also desirable, but thinwire has fairly serious length and number of node restrictions that may not present a satisfactory profile for usage. Twisted pair technologies could provide a solution, but again there are node limitations and length plus the twisted pair solution is somewhat noise sensitive. Fiber might also figure into a solution, but it is difficult to tap and currently expensive.

What's a company to do?

Some vendors have considered this and developed what is generically called "hub technology." Basically, a specialized repeater or bridge is used to interconnect Ethernet segments of differing media types. One such device on the market allows two thinwire segments, two thickwire segments, and two fiber segments to be connected to a hub box and all segments connected together in a method similar to a repeater between the differing segments. With this type of connection technology, varying types of Ethernet media can be used in a corporate or factory environment in an harmonious way.

The benefits are obvious. The ability to run, today, media and interconnection technology that makes sense in varying environments and later be able to connect to new types of media allows longevity of technology choice. This is especially true if other networks being considered fall under the 802 umbrella. With the use of hub technology for Ethernet media interconnection and the use of FDDI for backbone connections, 802 networks can easily grow and multiply as required by corporate need.

Some network vendors have begun to provide LAN networks that use Ethernet contention methods and mechanisms, but are not called "Ethernet" due to slight modifications or because of other technical or political reasons. In fact, the IBM PC Network product, while not "technically" an Ethernet because of its 4Mbps speed, does resemble, very strongly, a broadband Ethernet. It supports 72 connections and only allows a network to be 1000 feet in length, but it uses the CSMA/CD access method (in a manner similar to Ethernet) and is configured similarly to a broadband Ethernet. Through the use of a head end amplifier and directional "hubs," the PC Networks allows users to connect to a limited function broadband network and share resources such as disks, printers, files, etc...

Other types of hub adapters allow the interconnection of non-coax to coax Ethernet through the use of adapters called baluns. Off the back of a PC or other such system an RJ11 or RJ45 cable is connected to a similar plug in the wall or on a cable. On the other side of the plug is a BNC, TNC, or other such coaxial connector that allows connection to a coaxial cable plant. In this manner, a flexible cable plant can be configured. By usage of hubs of baluns or baluns adapters, star configuration topologies and other similar types of networks can be created.

Hub adapters are very important to Ethernet futures in other ways. Some PBX vendors are starting to incorporate the connectivity capabilities of Ethernet into the PBX system, allowing the PBX to serve as a hub and generalized message router on a single Ethernet or interconnecting multiple Ethernets. In this manner, the PBX could become the LAN for an organization, allowing many nodes to communicate transparently with each other over Ethernets connected through various PBX systems (baseband and broadband).

In summary, hub adapter technologies will become increasingly popular as more companies begin to implement Ethernets but wish to use existing wiring plants or will make use of AT&T-specified PDS or other such master wiring schemes. As building and business technologies change, so will Ethernet media access methods.

Effect of New Computational Architectures

The parallel computer is coming. Face up to it and be prepared to be ooo'd, ahh'd, and amazed. The sales force from your favorite computer vendor will be, so you might as well too.

All kidding aside, the parallel architecture computer presents the challenge to networking in a big way. With greater computational power comes more work in shorter amounts of time. It also means the ability to handle much higher resolution graphics than before with greater finesse and resolution. Needless to say, users will want to transfer such images around and display them in remote locations.

Greater computational power also means the ability to access larger amounts of data in a smoother, faster fashion. Incorporation of optical technology to storage technology means that small optical platters will be storing data in the order of gigabytes. All this will be accessed by various computers, further causing network incorporation to be critical to the solution of the overall computational problem.

With higher resolution graphics, better storage, and faster computers comes the problem of applications. Programs that are truly distributed (pieces of a program on various machines that are tied together) will become very popular. Imagine being able to place "hog-mode" (computationally intense) sections of program code on specific processors that can handle the load with other parts of the program residing on different machines. Sound farfetched? It's not. Already the beginnings of such systems are starting to emerge at the larger computer vendors and universities.

What does all of this have to do with Ethernet? Plenty. While Ethernet has traditionally been used for network-oriented data transmission such as program-to-program communications, file transfers, terminal access, shared disk, and shared printer resources, faster medium technology will lend itself well to faster Ethernets. As a matter to consider, look at current computer I/O bus speeds. Upon examination, you will find many of them are actually slower than the bandwidth speed of most baseband or broadband Ethernet. So the question really is, how long before Ethernet is used to replace a traditional computer bus?

Apparently not long. In fact, some companies such as Digital Equipment Corporation and 3COM have already started offering peripheral-less workstations that utilize Ethernet to access remotely located disks, tapes, terminals, printers, etc. In other words, the traditional computer bus on the local computer is effectively supplanted by the Ethernet network. The advantages to such a scheme are numerous: centralized access to data resources, shared peripherals between multiple systems, easy addition of additional computational horsepower without the overhead of adding peripherals to each new system since they share peripherals on existing systems, etc. Another advantage is in the area of management of resources. System managers can now control access to all peripherals as well as provide backup/restore facilities to users without having to go from machine to machine to perform same. Also, maintenance functions and costs are reduced as there are, quite literally, fewer moving parts.

To provide the usage of Ethernet as a computer interface bus is not difficult. Vendors, through software trickery, place a "smart" Ethernet controller in each system on the Ethernet that will be used in the "distributed system." With the controller is a section of ROM code that has enough software incorporated in it to allow the remote unit to send out a message requesting connection to a remote disk resource. If the system has not booted, the connection request will typically be for a system bootstrap and a remote system that knows how to send the proper software to the requesting node will respond to the request. The requesting node receives the proper load information and the remote boots itself. When the system is active, it "thinks" that the disks and tapes that it is accessing are local to the system; in reality they are located on the remote systems and are accessed through the Ethernet.

With the introduction of faster Ethernets and larger Ethernets, the concept of sharing peripherals and other resources will grow. Future systems will need the faster Ethernets to supply the access speeds necessary to provide adequate throughput for applications running on the network. Systems now that take up a desktop will eventually be the size of a 8.5"x11" book (along the Xerox "Dynabook" technology) and will plug into Ethernet wall adapters in a manner similar to the way that telephones are currently connected. Some vendors are even experimenting with the use of infra-red communications linkages which may eliminate the need for system-to-network cabling. As a result, a user may walk into a room, turn on his/her portable computer, and immediately be connected to an Ethernet, no matter where in the building the user is located. Since Ethernet is a broadcast-oriented technology, it does not matter where a node is located physically on the Ethernet as all nodes will be able to communicate with it. In the case described, the node has moved, but it does not matter.

Usage of more powerful computers that are less expensive brings the challenge of how data will be handled. With the usage of more powerful Ethernets and more powerful protocols and access technologies, Ethernet will provide very flexible and powerful communications topologies and solutions.

Chapter Summary

The future of Ethernet is bright and open. Connection to other 802-series networks through FDDI, connection to other network technologies such as IBM's Systems Network Architecture (SNA) through powerful gateways, and usage of other types of media such as fiber will all serve to increase the powerful draw to Ethernet. A proven technology, Ethernet is flexible enough in architecture to be considered for use in areas were deterministic networks typically are needed and versions of Ethernet are expected to provide such support. In short, the simplicity of architecture of Ethernet allows for a great many paths to be followed which will allow Ethernets to grow and provide service for a great many years to come.

Recommended Reading List

Digital Equipment Corp., Intel, Xerox. "The Ethernet: A Local Area Network: Data Link Layer and Physical Layer Specifications." Version 1.0. September, 1980.

Digital Equipment Corp., Intel, Xerox. "The Ethernet: A Local Area Network: Data Link Layer and Physical Layer Specifications." Version 2.0. November, 1982.

Archer, Rowland: "The Practical Guide to Local Area Networks." Berkeley, Ca.: Osborne McGraw-Hill, 1986.

Hammond, J.L and O'Reilly, P.J.P.: "Performance Analysis of Local Computer Networks." Reading, Ma.: Addison-Wesley Publishing Co., 1986.

R.M. Metcalf and D.R. Boggs: "Ethernet: Distributed Packet Switching for Local Computer Networks." Communications of the ACM 19, no. 7 (July 1976):394-404.

Stallings, W.: "Local Networks: An Introduction." New York, NY: Macmillan Publishing Co., 1984.

"IEEE Standard 802.2 - Logical Link Control Specification." Silver Springs, MD: IEEE Computer Society, DEC. 1982.

"IEEE Standard 802.3 - CSMA/CD Access Methods and Physical Layer Specifications." Silver Springs, MD: IEEE Computer Society, 1985.

"IEEE Standard 802.4 - Token Passing Bus Access Method and Physical Layer Specifications." Silver Springs, MD: IEEE Computer Society, 1982.

Abramson, N.: "The ALOHA System." Computer-Communications Networks. Englewood Cliffs, N.J.: Prentice-Hall, 1973.

Tanenbaum, A.S.: "Computer Networks." Englewood Cliffs, N.J.: Prentice-Hall, 1981.

Cooper, E.: "Broadband Network Technology: An Overview for the Data and Telecommunications Industries." Mountain View, Ca.: Sytek Press, 1986.

Jordan, L.E. and Churchill, B.: "Communications and Networking for the IBM PC." Bowie, MD.: Robert J. Brady Co., 1983.

Purser, M.: "Data Communications for Programmers." Wokingham, England: Addison-Wesley Publishing Co., 1986.

Kleeman, M., Anderson, B., Angermeyer, J., Fisher, S., and McCoy, S.: "PC LAN Primer." Indianapolis, IN.: Howard W. Sams & Co., 1987.

Chorafas, D.: "Designing and Implementing Local Area Networks." New York, NY: McGraw-Hill Book Co., 1984.

Digital Equipment Corporation, "DECnet Digital Network Architecture Phase IV Ethernet Data Link Functional Specification." Maynard, MA.: Digital Equipment Corporation, 1983.